A SPECIAL OFFER.
WHITE LEGHORNS
Hatching Eggs
from all pens 6/6 doz
Hatch House
Poultry Farm.

G. CHURCHILL, MA... HA... ...ELL
Groceries & Provisions
Cigarettes & Tobacco.
COOKED HAM. BEST BUTTER
AND BACON A SPECIALITY

Telephones:
Southend 450, London: Royal 3798
We deliver **FLOWERS**
to all parts of
THE WORLD.

NURSE VOKES,
Certified General
& Maternity Nurse
"GLENWOOD"
HOCKLEY RISE.

G. H. Willans & Sons
Exchange Stores
Special this week
Local New Laid Eggs
from 1/3 Dozen
West Street Rochford
Telephone Rochford 44

Hockley and District.
BRITISH LEGION
A MEETING WILL BE
HELD IN THE
Wesleyan Hall,
HOCKLEY.
FOR MEMBERS ONLY.
Tuesday April 17th.
at 8p.m.
Chairman Dr. A. L. Dobbyn

H. J. Arthy,
Fancy Bread and
Biscuit Baker,
Pastrycook & Confectioner
High Street, OCHFORD.
High Road, HOCKLEY

Teas & Light Refreshments.
Wedding Birthday Christening Cakes
Telephone 45.

Hockley Wesleyan
Sports Club
Ground Highams Road,
Membership is open to all
Fees: Tennis
Ladies 15/-
Gentlemen 21/-
Bowls 15/- Many vacancies
Full Particulars from
Hon Secretary: "LYNSTAN;;
Hawkwell Road,

G. A. Thorpe & Sons,
SHEEPOTES,
Hockley - - Essex
COAL & COKE
Merchants.
Special prices for
Large Orders.
Cartage Contractors
Join our Coal Club NOW

Hockley Battery Works.
High Tension Batteries. Hand
Batteries, Fresh Stock only,
ENGLAND-RICHARDS Process
P S. Murray, Longsight,
High Road, Hockley.

Moderate Fees
Miss F, M, Hayward, G.S M.
Visits and Receives pupils
Pianoforte & Theory, Violin Taught
Francis Farm, Near Station Hockley,

Marigold Corner Cafe,
Hockley
TEAS & LIGHT REFRESHMENTS
Whist Drive Held
Saturday Apr. 14th. 7-30
1/6 Including Refreshments.
TELEPHONE 50 Hockley

Hockley, Hullbridge & Hawkwell Past

The *Spa Hotel*, Hockley, *c*.1910.

Hullbridge Ferry, *c*.1920.

Hawkwell village centre.

Hockley, Hullbridge & Hawkwell Past

Lesley Vingoe

Phillimore

1999

Published by
PHILLIMORE & CO. LTD.
Shopwyke Manor Barn, Chichester, West Sussex

ISBN 1 86077 110 6

Printed and bound in Great Britain by
BIDDLES LTD.
Guildford, Surrey

Contents

Dedicated to my mother Jessie Kathleen Johnson (1914-1997)
who fostered in me her love of the past
and with many thanks to my husband and family
for their support and encouragement,
without which this book would never have been written

List of Illustrations

Frontispiece: The *Spa Hotel*, Hockley, *c*.1910; Hullbridge Ferry, *c*.1920; Hawkwell village centre

Acknowledgements

The author wishes to thank the following for permission to reproduce illustrations: Allied Domecq, 68; Barney's Pet Shop, 121; Mr. James Bowen, 32, 99, 100; British Library, 27; Mrs. Celia Burt, 113, 114; Mr. Victor Bundick, 101, 111; Colin and Gloria Burwell, 93; Mrs. Jenny Church, 5; David Collins, 26; Sue and Royston Dean, 60, 61, 102, 124; Essex County Council, frontispiece—Hullbridge Ferry, 2, 3, 58, 83, 98, 103, 104, 149; Mr. John Frankland, 66; Hockley Parish Council, 130; Mr. Alan Holder, 9; Miss Gladys Horslin, 19, 33, 39, 56, 70, 86, 126; Miss Joan Hurrell, 14, 151; Mrs. Nan Kemp, 146; Phillimore & Co. Ltd., 1, 4; Mr. Brian O'Shea, 8; Mr. Dennis Potter, 45, 46, 55, 71, 72, 73, 77-79, 86, 94, 118, 119; Mrs. Pat Read, 143; Rochford District Council, 139; Father Richard Seabrook, 17; Mrs. Shelley, 40, 108; Mrs. Sheila Stock, 145; Mr. Paul Taylor, 59, 91, 128; Mrs. Elizabeth Wakefield, 129, 131; The Warden and Fellows of Wadham College, Oxford, 28; Southend Borough Council, 59, 63, 65, 67, 76, 97, 106, 122, 132, 133, 135. All other photographs are from the author's private collection.

Particular thanks to Patrick Cabell for his drawings of Plumberow Manor House, no. 5, and the structure of a timber-framed house in the 16th century, no 25. To Maurice Wakeham, Librarian at Anglia Polytechnic University, for explaining the complexities of copyright. To the staff of Essex Record Office, Chelmsford and Southend (especially Sarah Ball), and Ken Crowe of the Southend Borough Council Museums Service. Also to my friend and neighbour, Margaret Pleate for her support and for proof reading the document.

To the following people and organisations I owe grateful thanks for providing me with historical information on the area: The Trustees, Hockley Public Hall; Hockley Parish Council; Hawkwell Parish Council; Wendy Sargent, Hockley Evangelical Church; Canon Williams, St Andrew's Rochford; The parish of St Mary's Hawkwell; Councillor Shirley James; Mr. Manly of the Rochford Hundred Historical Society and Mrs. L. Jerram-Burrows.

There is one person who has contributed more than anyone else to the content of this book, and I would in particular like to thank Miss Glady Horslin, born and bred in Hockley and still resident in the village, whose stories about herself, family and the people of old Hockley gave me an invaluable insight into a way of life that has gone for ever.

Last but not least, thanks indeed to my husband Richard for his support and encouragement through all the long and sometimes arduous weeks of writing.

Introduction

THE ORIGINS of Hockley, Hawkwell and Hullbridge are unknown. It was the coming of the railway in 1889 that changed things for ever. Hockley, always the largest of the settlements, was originally a scattered agricultural community that grew into a commuter town following the arrival of the railway. The Domesday manor of Hockley also held lands at Paglesham and the marshes between Clements Green Creek and Fen Creek at South Woodham Ferrers on the north bank of the river. Although some two miles away, the riverside settlement of Hullbridge was also part of the parish of Hockley. Like Hockley, Hawkwell, also mentioned in Domesday Book, relied heavily on agriculture and its small population clustered around the two main farms of Clements Hall and Golden Cross, located at either end of the parish.

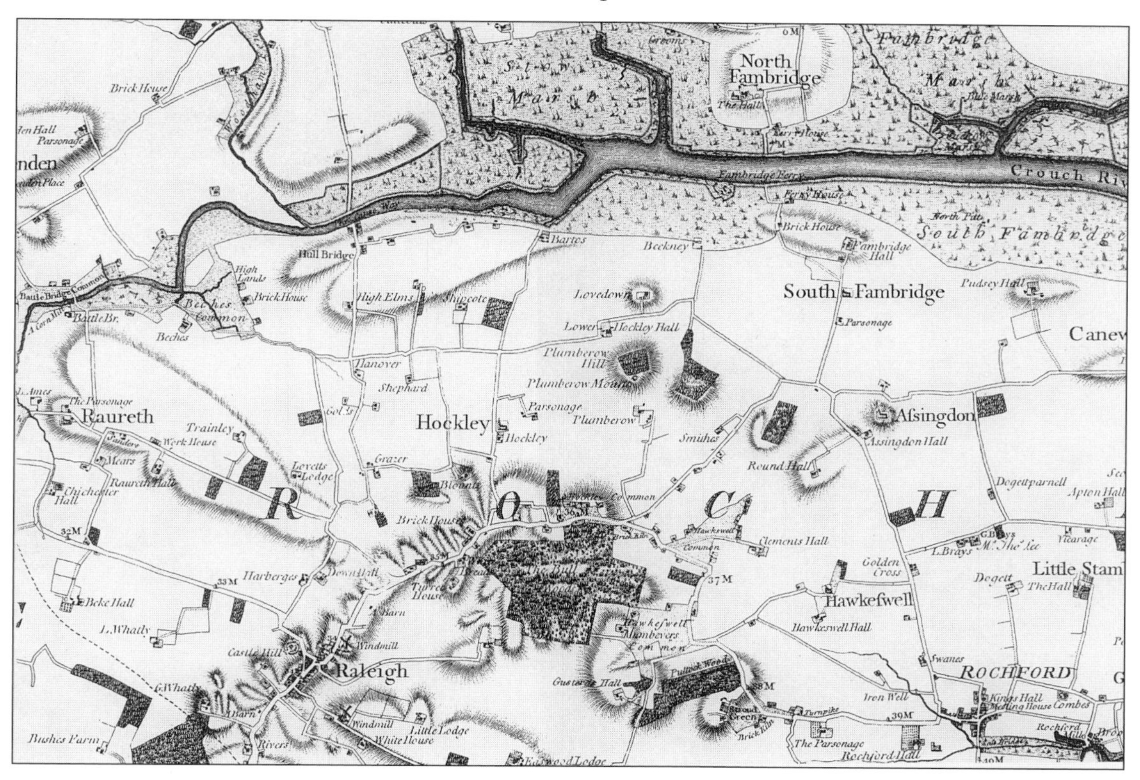

1 Chapman and André's map of the Hockley, Hawkwell and Hullbridge area, 1777.

The history of Hockley, Hawkwell and Hullbridge is the story of ordinary people doing their best to make a living from the land. Although it is possible that the Battle of Ashingdon was fought nearby, no recorded engagements of national importance took place locally. Nor did any rich and famous people make their homes in the area.

The land was difficult to work and the lack of clean drinking water was a very real problem. The climate in the lower lying areas was dank and unhealthy and life expectancy was short. The 'ague', a form of malaria, was prevalent and it was not until well into this century that the last of the marshes were drained and the malarial mosquito was eradicated.

Until 1968, when it broke away from Hockley and became a parish in its own right, Hullbridge's history ran parallel to that of Hockley. Therefore, unless stated otherwise, all references to Hockley also included Hullbridge.

It was the pretty countryside around Hockley that caught the eye of the early photographers and thousands of postcards were produced to sell to day trippers who arrived by train and charabanc from London and Southend. There are therefore many more photographs of Hockley in this book than of either Hawkwell or Hullbridge. The photographers, to a lesser degree, turned their attention to Hullbridge when it gained popularity as a riverside resort. However, old photographs of Hawkwell are very rare indeed as it unfortunately lacked the physical attractions of either Hockley or Hullbridge.

Chapter One

The Early History

HULLBRIDGE HAS EVIDENCE of the earliest settlement in our area. A stone axe and arrowheads have been collected from the foreshore. Many microliths, tiny pieces of worked flint used to make knives and implements, have also been found, which suggests that at one time a flint factory existed in the area. During the period 7,000–4,000 B.C. the settlers left their riverside homes to hack out small fields from the wooded hills above the river and to practise their new-found farming skills. These small communities would eventually grow into the Hockley and Hawkwell of today.

The deep ploughing that has taken place over the years has inevitably destroyed any evidence of earlier settlement. However, Oliver Rackham in his book *History of the Countryside* is of the opinion that a strong administration existed in the area during the Iron Age. This is indicated by the semi-regular roads and field grids of the Dengie and Rochford peninsulas which align across the estuary and are today still identifiable on maps.

There is, however, one permanent reminder of our ancient past—Plumberow Mount, in Hockley. The Mount is a tumulus set on a hill overlooking the Crouch valley and was excavated in 1913 by a group of enthusiastic antiquarians who called themselves the 'Morant Society'. They had hoped to find a rich royal burial like the one which had recently been excavated on Mersea Island. Three trenches were cut into the mount, meeting at the centre, where a wooden post was discovered. Sadly for the Morant Society, the only treasure that came to light was one Roman coin dated A.D. 48 and some shards of Roman and Saxon pottery! The Mount's true purpose was never determined and remains a mystery to this day. It has been suggested that it was one of the Romano/British signalling stations set up to protect the Saxon Shore after the Romans left Britain. Alternatively, it could have been a pagan religious site as it was not unusual for heathen altars to be set up on high places. In fact, Christian priests were instructed to build their churches on the sites of heathen sanctuaries; it is very noticeable that, with the exception of Hawkwell, all the ancient churches in the area are built on hills!

Although the road to South Fambridge is believed to be Roman, no other evidence of Roman occupation has been found in the area. However, there is a well defined series of boundary banks in Hockley Woods, which could date back to Roman times.

1066 and the Battle of Hastings saw the end of the English monarchy and the imposition of a new order based on land ownership, known as the feudal system. The victorious Norman King William rewarded his supporters with the estates of the vanquished English on which they in their turn placed their own tenants to keep law and order in the area. Officially called 'manors', in the vast majority of cases these landholdings were little more than large farms. The Saxon method of grouping villages into hundreds for administrative purposes was retained, and Hockley and Hawkwell continued as two of the 24 villages that made up the Rochford Hundred. In 1086 the Domesday Survey was completed, to ascertain just who held what, from whom and where.

Both Hockley and Hawkwell appear in Domesday Book. Hockley is spelt variously as Hacheleia, Hocheleiam and Hocheleia, and Hawkwell as Hacuuella, Hechuuella and Hacheuuella. Experts believe that Hockley's name may have derived from the ownership of a field, in Old English a ley, by a man or family group called Hocca. Alternatively, it might simply refer to a high pasture. There was a long-held belief that Hawkwell is Old German for 'high well' and refers to the stream that once ran across the upper common. However, it is now accepted that the village got its name from the brook that runs by the church, at which point it bends, causing a hook or 'hacca'. The 'well' simply refers to the stream as a water supply. Hullbridge had to wait until 1375 before it was officially mentioned, when the settlement was referred to as Whoulebrigg—the 'brigg', Old English for bridge, over the river 'Whoule', as the Crouch was then known.

Domesday Book tells us that the king's friend and supporter, Swein, who lived at Rayleigh Castle, held two manors in Hockley, probably in the vicinity of lower Plumberow. Two Frenchmen, Godbold and Odo, tenanted one of the estates which later became known as Little Hockley Hall. A man called Payne had a much larger property, believed to be the original, and still existing, Lower Hockley Hall.

Although only remembered as a road name nowadays, in the 11th century Plumberow was a small hamlet and appears twice in Domesday Book. Spelt as Plumbga and Plubga, the larger of the two landholdings also belonged to Swein and was occupied by a tenant called Ascelin. The other reference is to a small plot of land which formed part of the vast estates of William de Warenne, the king's brother-in-law, and was tenanted by a smallholder named Ranulf. The entry is brief, but we are told that Ranulf obtained the land by exchanging it for some in Normandy.

The largest and most important manor in Hockley belonged to St Mary's Abbey at Barking, and had done so since before the Norman Conquest. With a population of approximately 160 people, its lands extended beyond Hullbridge to the north bank of the river Crouch. The entry also mentions a small piece of land which William of Boursigny, probably the village priest, held from the church. At the reformation all the lands of the abbey became the property of the Crown. In 1539 Henry VIII granted the manor to Thomas Cromwell, until he fell out of favour when it reverted to the Crown. Queen Mary, in 1557, granted it to Sir Richard Rich, who put in as tenant Edmund Tyrell. At that time the manor was worth £53 6s. 8d. per annum. It remained the property of the Rich family until the death of Charles, Earl of Warwick, in 1673 when it passed to Essex, second daughter of Robert, Lord Rich. She in turn conveyed it to her husband Daniel, Earl of Nottingham. Eventually the estate was sold to Wadham College, Oxford. The present Hockley Hall, itself an ancient building, is opposite the church. However, the exact location of the original manor house is uncertain, as in some early documents and maps it is shown on the other side of the road next to the church.

Both the Hockley and Plumberow entries contain references to mills. However, they would not have been windmills, but tidemills, built way out on the marshes to harness the power of the tide. The first reference to a windmill, as we would understand it today, appears in the manorial records of 1590; the mill was located in Church Road.

In Hawkwell Godfrey held a small plot of land, once again from Swein. Two other entries refer to land that had belonged to an Englishman by the name of Wulfmer, which at the Conquest was given to King William's

steward, Eudo Dapifer. Eudo passed one parcel of land to Pirot whose manor has been identified as Hawkwell Hall, which still stands opposite the church. The Pirot family's occupation is well documented and they remained at Hawkwell well into the 14th century. Eudo kept the other portion of land for himself and built his manor on what is now Clements Hall.

Nearly all the Hockley and Hawkwell entries in Domesday Book refer to large flocks of sheep and goats. Why so many? In the days before field drainage the area was very marshy, particularly near the river which was not banked and therefore prone to flooding. Cattle cannot survive in wet conditions, but sheep and goats can. Not only were sheep important for their meat and wool, but also for dairy products and Essex cheeses were famous well into the 17th century. A brief note, dated 1635, appears in the records of Hockley manor in which the Archbishop of Canterbury thanks the tenant for a supply of cheeses. There were also many pigs who would have fed on acorns in the woods.

2 Plumberow Mount, Hockley, prior to excavation in 1913. The little house on the top is a summerhouse.

3 Plumberow Mount, Hockley, during excavation by the Morant Society.

4 Domesday Book was commissioned by King William in 1086, as a statistical survey of England. It shows the population and productive resources of the country, their value and who held them. The entries show England as it existed before the Norman Conquest in 1066 and the situation 20 years later.

Hund de Rochefort. Hocheleiā ten& sēp. s. ɱ. p ɱ. 7. vii. hid 7. dim. Tē xxiiii. uilt. m. xxvii. sēp. xii. bor. Tē. iii. ser. m. null. Sēp. ii. car in dnio. 7. xv. car hom. past. cc. ou. i. mol. ii. runc. viii. an. cli. ou. xxvi. por. Sēp ual. x. lib. De hoc man ten& Witt de burfigni de eccta. iii. uirg. 7. i. car. 7 ual. xxi. sol. in eod. ptio.

Hundred of ROCHFORD
St. Mary's has always held HOCKLEY as a manor; 7½ hides.
Then 24 villagers, now 27; always 12 smallholders; then 3 slaves, now none. Always 2 ploughs in lordship; 15 men's ploughs.
Pasture, 200 sheep; 1 mill. 2 cobs, 8 cattle, 151 sheep, 26 pigs.
Value always £10.
Of this manor, William of Boursigny holds 3 virgates from the Church. 1 plough.
Value 21s in the same assessment.

(a) The manor of Hockley, known to have been in the vicinity of SS Peter and Paul Church. Possibly the present Hockley Hall in Church Road.

Hocheleiam tenent. ii. franci de Sueno. Godebold. i. hid. 7 Odo. xxx. ac. 7 hoc Man tenuit. i. lib ho. t. r. e. Sēp. ii. car. 7. dim. in dnio. Tē. iii. bord. m. v. Tē. v. ser. m. iii. Past. c. ou Sēp. i. mol. Tē. v. an. 7. x. porc. 7. c. ou. 7. vii. cap. M. i. runc. 7. xiii. an. 7 xxii. porc. 7. c. ou. 7. iiii. uasa ap. Tē ual. xxx. sol. P 7 m. xl.

2 Frenchmen hold HOCKLEY from Swein, Godbold (holds) 1 hide and Odo 30 acres. 1 free man held this manor before 1066.
Always 2½ ploughs in lordship.
Then 3 smallholders, now 5; then 5 slaves, now 3.
Pasture, 100 sheep; always 1 mill. Then 5 cattle, 10 pigs, 100 sheep and 7 goats; now 1 cob, 13 cattle, 22 pigs, 100 sheep and 4 beehives.
Value then 30s; later and now 40[s].

(b) Believed to have been what later became known as Little Hockley Hall. Its exact location, somewhere in the lower Plumberow area, is not known. The present Little Hockley Hall is a modern building.

Hacheleiā ten& Pagan de. S. p. i. ɱ. 7. p. i. hid. Sēp. xii. bord. 7. i. car. in dnio. Tē. ii. car. hom. m. i. Silu. xxx. porc. Past. cc. ou. M. i. mol. Tē. ii. runc. 7. ii. an. 7. xii. porc. 7. clx. ou. 7. xxx. cap. m. iiii. runc. x. an. xxiiii. porc. ccc. ou. liii. cap.

Payne holds HOCKLEY from Swein as 1 manor, for 1 hide.
Always 12 smallholders; 1 plough in lordship. Then 2 men's ploughs, now 1.
Woodland, 30 pigs; pasture, 200 sheep; now 1 mill. Then 2 cobs, 2 cattle, 12 pigs, 160 sheep and 30 goats; now 4 cobs, 10 cattle, 24 pigs, 300 sheep, 53 goats, 6 beehives.
Value then £3; now [£] 4.

(c) Lower Hockley Hall, Lower Road, Hockley.

(**d**) Plumberow Manor (now demolished).

Plumbḡa ten& Idē . A . de . S . qđ tenuit Rob fili Wimarcæ . p . m̄ . 7 . p . I . hid . Tc̄ . I . borđ . 7 . I . ser . m̄ . VIII . bor . Tc̄ . I . car 7 dim in dn̄io . m̄ . I . dim . car . hom . Silu . XXX . porc . Past . C . ou . m̄ . I . mol . Tc̄ . I . runc . VII . an . XXX . porc . C . ou . XL . cap . m̄ . II . runc . 7 . I . pull . III . an . XX . porc . C . ou . XXIII . cap . Tc̄ uat . XX . sol . m̄ . XL .

A(scelin) also holds PLUMBEROW from Swein, which Robert son of Wymarc held as a manor, for 1 hide.
Then 1 smallholder and 1 slave; now 8 smallholders. Then 1½ ploughs in lordship, now 1. ½ men's plough.
Woodland, 30 pigs; pasture, 100 sheep; now 1 mill. Then 1 cob, 7 cattle, 30 pigs, 100 sheep, 40 goats; now 2 cobs, 1 foal, 3 cattle, 20 pigs, 100 sheep, 23 goats.
Value then 20s; now 40[s].

(**e**) An unknown location in Plumberow. Eventually incorporated into Plumberow Manor.

In Plūbga . ten& Ranulf de W . XXX . ac . qđ . ten . I . lib . hō . t . r . e Tc̄ dim . car . m̄ . I . Tc̄ . V . sol . m̄ . X . has tras reclamat . pro escangio de normannia.

In PLUMBEROW Ranulf holds 30 acres from William, which 1 free man held before 1066. Then ½ plough, now 1.
[Value] then 5s; now 10[s].
He claims these lands by exchange in Normandy.

(**f**) Clements Hall in Hawkwell.

Hunđ de Rochefort . ~~Hacuuella ten& . E . in dn̄io .~~ qđ tenuit Vlmar . lib hō . p . m̄ . 7 . ~~P . III . hid . 7 . dim .~~ XV . ac . min . t . r . e . Tc̄ . XI . uilt . m̄ . VIII . Sēp . V . borđ . Tc̄ . II . ser . m̄ . III . Sēp . II . car . in dnio . Tc̄ . VI . car . hoūm m̄ . V . IIII . ac . pti . Silu . X . porc . Tc̄ . II . runc . m̄ . VI . Tc̄ . V . anim . m̄ . XVI . Tc̄ . CII . ou . m̄ . CVI . Sēp . XX . porc . m̄ . II . uasa apū . Tc̄ uat . VI . lib . m̄ . VII .

Hundred of ROCHFORD
Eudo holds HAWKWELL in lordship which Wulfmer, a free man, held as a manor, for 3½ hides less 15 acres before 1066.
Then 11 villagers, now 8; always 5 smallholders. Then 2 slaves, now 3. Always 2 ploughs in lordship. Then 6 men's ploughs, now 5.
Meadow, 4 acres; woodland, 10 pigs. Then 2 cobs, now 6; then 5 cattle, now 16; then 102 sheep, now 106; always 20 pigs; now 2 beehives.
Value then £6; now [£] 7.

(**g**) Hawkwell Hall, Hawkwell, is opposite St Mary's Church in Rectory Road.

Hunđ de Rochefort. Hechuuellā ten& Pirot de . Eudone qđ ten Vlmer . t . r . e . p Man . 7 . p . III . hid . 7 . dim . XV . ac . min . Tc̄ . XI . uilti . m̄ VIII . Sēp . V . borđ . Tc̄ . II . ser . m̄ . III . Sēp . II . car . in dn̄io . Tc̄ . VI . car . hominū . m̄ V . IIII . ac . pti . Silu . X . porc . Tc̄ . II . runc . 7 . V . an . CII . ou . XX . porc . m̄ . XVI . an . CVI . ou . XX . porc . II . uasa apū . Tc̄ 7 p uat . VI . lib . m̄ . VII .

Hundred of ROCHFORD
11 Pirot holds HAWKWELL from Eudo, which Wulfmer held before 1066 as a manor, for 3½ hides less 15 acres.
Then 11 villagers, now 8; always 5 smallholders. Then 2 slaves, now 3. Always 2 ploughs in lordship. Then 6 men's ploughs, now 5.
Meadow, 4 acres; woodland, 10 pigs. Then 2 cobs, 5 cattle, 102 sheep, 20 pigs; now 16 cattle, 106 sheep, 20 pigs, 2 beehives.
Value then and later £6; now [£] 7.

5 Line drawing taken from a now lost photograph of Plumberow Manor prior to its demolition in 1960.

Many ancient farms still exist in the locality such as Blounts (1453), Pickerells (1579), Coventry Farm (1523), Boxes (1403), Highlands (1412) and Bartons, first mentioned in 1500. However, the present farmhouse dates from the beginning of this century as the original building, much nearer the river, was destroyed by fire. Lovedown and Sheepcotes farms also have long histories. In the grounds of Sheepcotes Farm it is possible to see the ridges and furrows left by the old method of ploughing.

By the middle ages Plumberow had become a sizeable hamlet having grown to include the other Domesday manors in the vicinity. In 1470 it formed part of the vast landholdings of William Tyrell, who stipulated in his will that the manor should be responsible for paying for a priest and schoolmaster at Rawreth.

The manor changed hands many times over the centuries' gradually decreasing in importance until it became nothing more than a farm. An estate manager's report dating from the early years of the last century states that the house had been painted, white washed and papered in a neat manner. As the tenant had not had enough boards for the weather boarding they had been procured for him. Two new doors were needed as well as 200 plain tiles and 600 bricks for repairing the roof and foundations. The tenant was also ordered to take one oak pollard (oak tree) for the repair of the fences to the pig styes. The front gate needed an iron lock and the fence required attention. An inventory was taken of the stock, from which we learn that there were 12 horses on the farm, all of whom are named and their ages recorded. To name just four: Violet was a 9-year-old brown mare,

Major a 4-year-old chestnut, Duke a 13-year-old bay and Jolly Boy a 10-year-old gelding. In 1869 Plumberow farm was advertised in *The Times* as

> consisting of a substantial and neat brick built house with buildings in good repair, pleasantly sheltered under rising ground called Plumberough Mount, with grass paddocks, 14 acres in front and nearly 310 acres of excellent corn land.

Printed particulars could be obtained from the *Golden Lion*, Rayleigh and the *Kings Head*, Rochford. The then tenant paid £426 per annum for the farm. Sadly, the old manor fell on increasingly hard times and was demolished in 1960, when an application was made for a caravan park on the site. Fortunately the application was refused and a housing development and the Apex shops built instead.

The old Hawkwell Hall was demolished and rebuilt in 1833. In 1866 the Hall was auctioned and the sales particulars give us an idea of how the building looked at that time. On the ground floor there was an entrance hall, servants hall, kitchen, pantries and offices. Upstairs there were six bedchambers and a dressing room with a separate servants' staircase. Outside was a brewhouse, coal house, knife house, chaise house and stable. There were five yards, each with a well and the usual farm yard buildings such as a granary, piggeries, stables, etc. The estate also included another smaller farm towards Ashingdon where there were also three cottages.

Clements Hall is far older and takes its name from Philip Clements, who lived there in 1440. Philip Clements' daughter married John Ingoe and the estate remained in the family

6 Manor Cottage, once part of the Hockley manor estate, was demolished to make way for Manor Road, Hockley. It is said to date from before the 17th century and to have contained a secret room.

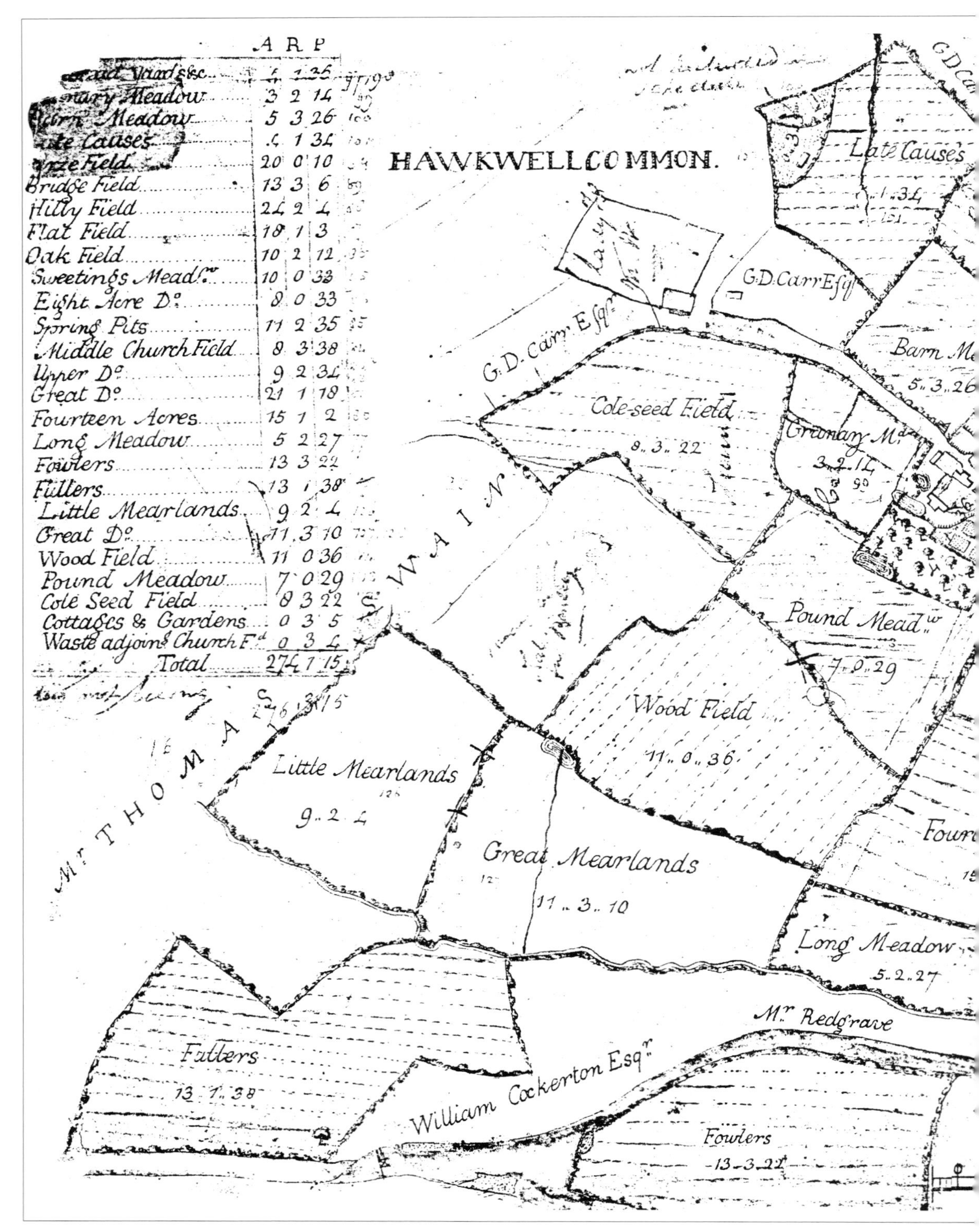

7 A map dated 1809 showing the Clements Hall estate, Hawkwell, then owned by Thomas Holt White. The house and outbuildings is in the middle, just off centre. Note the tiny drawing of St Mary's Church on Rectory Road at the bottom of the map.

CLEMENTS HALL
Manor Farm
in the Parish of
HAWKWELL ESSE
belonging to
Thos Holt White
1809.
Mr H Townsend.
Revd Mr Wise
Hilly Field
24. 2. 4
Bridge Field
13. 3. 6
Oak Field
10. 2. 12
Flat Field
18. 1. 3
G D Carr Esqr
Upr Church Field
9. 2. 34
Bristow Esqr
Spring Pits
11. 2. 35
Midle Church Field
8. 3. 38
Great Church Field
21. 1. 19
10. 0. 33
W
E
10
15
20

8 A photograph taken in the last few years of Clements Hall, Hawkwell.

9 Clements Hall lodge seen here during development of the area when it was used as the estate office, *c.*1920.

10 Lower Hockley Hall, *c.*1950.

until 1604 when it was sold to Richard Rich, Earl of Warwick. A sizeable estate, the entrance road originally crossed the common before passing through gates which were removed when the parish became responsible for the repair of the highway in the last century. However, the lodge still remains. When the estate lands were sold off for development the old building deteriorated rapidly. It had many owners and at one time was used as an orphanage. Fortunately this ancient house is now in safe hands.

Life at Lower Hockley Hall could never have been easy for the original inhabitants of this lovely old building. Being close to the river and the unhealthy marshes, the land was difficult to work and required considerable drainage and manuring. In the first quarter of the 19th century, Philip Hicks, the then tenant, paid out £2,000 on drainage and manure, and in one year carted 4,000 loads of earth and laid 1,000 loads of chalk on 11 acres in an effort to improve the soil.

Both Hockley and Hawkwell had commons on which the local people could graze their animals and collect firewood. Hockley lost its common in the 18th century when it was enclosed to form Betts Farm. Hawkwell, on the other hand, had two commons: the upper common, the remains of which fronts the *White Hart Inn*, and the lower common, long since turned into farmland in the Mount Bovers area. For many years the people of Hockley made use of the Poors Land, later known as Spa Meadow, along the Southend Road as an open space and common until that inevitably vanished under housing.

In medieval times salt making was an important industry along the river Crouch, especially on the north bank of the river, formerly in the parish of Hockley. The salt crystals were produced by evaporating salt water in huge earthenware pans over fires. Over the years the mounds of broken pans, baked earth and rubbish grew until, their origins forgotten,

11 A relatively recent photograph of Hockley Hall, Church Road, Hockley.

they became known as St Thomas' Hills and later 'red hills'. In the 19th century they were the cause of considerable speculation amongst antiquarians who excavated them and declared them to be the funeral pyres of Saxon warriors killed in the Battle of Ashingdon in 1016!

An intriguing will exists from 1547 when John Creke, weller of Hockley, stated that he left

> his wyff a seame and a half of whet, half a seame of malte, half a barell of butter, halfe a way of cheyse, upon condition that she depart from the house after his decease, or between this and Michaelmas, but if she remayne there untill Michaelmas, then her legacy of whet, malte, butter and chese to be voide and of none effect.

The final clause is also a curious one:

> That eche of my sones shall be ruled by th'other and yf any of them be stubborn or sturdy and will not be ruled by his brethren and myne ov'seres shall forfitt £20 to his bretheren, or his parte of goods as my will is.

Poor lady. One wonders what she had done to deserve such a family!

Chapter Two

Worship and Praise

BOTH HOCKLEY AND HAWKWELL are fortunate in possessing small but beautiful and historic parish churches. The residents of Hullbridge, however, were expected to travel to Hockley for the sake of their souls. In the medieval period there is mention of a chapel dedicated to St Thomas a Becket at Hullbridge, the remains of which have long since vanished. The chapel was originally built by the river crossing and it was here that pilgrims, on their way to either Canterbury or Walsingham, would stop to pray for a safe journey. In recent years a new parish church has been erected and proudly bears the name of the old chapel.

Set on a hill overlooking the lovely Crouch valley, Hockley's parish church is dedicated to SS Peter and Paul. Although mentioned in Domesday Book, no vestige of that original building remains. In 1220 it was rebuilt and enlarged, when a chancel chapel and the beautiful north arcade were added. The font of Purbeck marble dates from 1160 and was hidden for many years in the tower while

12 View from Hockley church across the Crouch valley, *c.*1920. The view has changed little over the years since this photograph was taken in the 1920s. The house in the centre is the vicarage. The original vicarage was built on the 'pightle', or church land, where now the old school house stands.

13 Early photograph of SS Peter and Paul, Hockley, showing the north colonnade. Note the oil lamps and 'pot bellied' stove to the fore of the picture.

14 Interior of SS Peter and Paul, Hockley, showing the 11th-century font.

a wooden bowl was used instead for baptisms. The tower, built in 1350, is unusual, having two stages. The first stage is square and the second octagonal.

Until the reformation the living or advowson—the right to appoint the priest—was in the gift of Barking Abbey and a rector looked after the needs of the small scattered population, supported by the tithes they paid and the produce of the church's land. In 1380 things were going badly for the abbey. Its income had been greatly reduced when the grazing lands it owned along the Thames were inundated. In an effort to improve the abbey's financial situation, the abbess appointed herself rector, which meant that Hockley's tithes were paid to her. She then appointed a vicar who received an income just sufficient to live on.

With the reformation the living passed from St Mary's Abbey, Barking, to the crown and then to Thomas Cromwell. It eventually came into the possession of Lord Petre at Ingatestone Hall. In 1695 Dorothy Wadham, Lord Petre's daughter, gave it to the college her husband had recently founded at Oxford—Wadham College.

Never a rich parish, Hockley suffered badly from absent incumbents. In 1565 the vicar is recorded as living in Kirby Kendal and in 1810 his successor resided at Salisbury. There are constant references to the bad state of repair of the building, and in 1690 snow was coming in through the roof. Evidence of colour on the walls was found during restoration in 1843, but was too faint to preserve. Further restoration took place in 1936 when two piscina and a holy water basin were uncovered, as well as the remains of the rood stairway and the original mensa or High altar was found under the floor.

Set into the ground immediately outside the Elizabethan brick porch, which dates from approximately 1580, is a coffin shaped stone bearing the initials of WW and dated 1791.

15 Unusual view of SS Peter and Paul, Hockley, taken from the graveyard from which can clearly be seen the octagonal tower and Tudor porch.

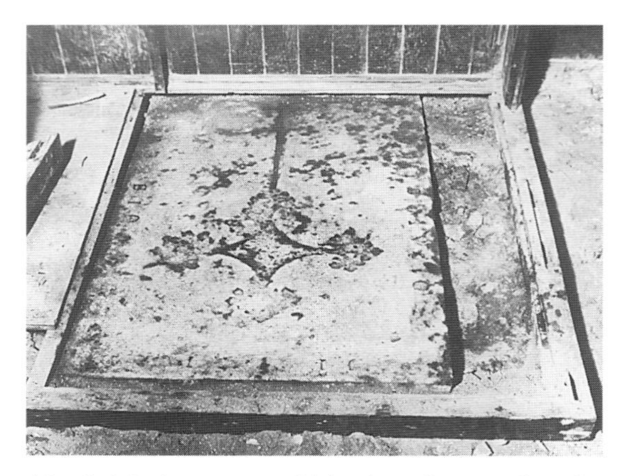

16 Original mensa or high altar discovered under the floor during restoration work in 1936.

This is said to be the grave of William Waight who left instructions that he was to be buried outside the church door; having been 'trampled' on in life, he wished to receive the same treatment after death!

The saddest story of all is that of William Tyms, deacon and curate of Hockley, who was burnt at the stake at Smithfield in April 1556 for heresy, having preached against the catholic doctrine of Queen Mary Tudor. A popular preacher, he was hidden in the district and gave two sermons at Plumberow Mount to over 100 people, but was eventually betrayed. During his imprisonment and torture, at one stage in the Bishop of London's coal hole, Tyms continued to write encouraging letters to his congregation in his own blood.

17 Visiting clergy and choirs attending to celebrate the Assumption of the Blessed Virgin Mary during the incumbency of Canon Morgan in the 1930s.

In the small window in the Lady Chapel there are six panes of glass in the form of a cross and bearing the words 'Deus ictus'—God stricken. How old they are or to what they relate is not known, but the message they carry is certainly poignant. It has been suggested that they refer to an outbreak of the plague. However, historical sources contain no reference to the plague having visited Hockley, or any of the surrounding area.

Hockley is fortunate in possessing some fine old ecclesiastical silver, stored for safe keeping in the local bank. However, its greatest treasure, although not in monetary value, is a very badly eroded block of stone carved with a barely discernible crucifix. When the tower was renovated recently the stone, which was built in above the west door, was removed and is at the time of writing with the Victoria and Albert Museum awaiting restoration. The experts advise that it is alabaster, probably of the 14th century, and once formed the centre panel of a triptych. It may even have been part of the original pre-reformation altar of the church.

The tiny parish church of St Mary the Virgin, Hawkwell has been successfully extended within the last few years to make it large enough to serve its current community. The original building dates back to approximately 1300, although there is the likelihood that it too has its roots in the 11th century. The nave was built in the 13th century and the chancel added sometime in the 14th century. In the 15th century the chancel was altered and a bell tower was added, standing on four oak posts with cross beams and curved braces supporting the square frame of the turret. The door is of particular interest as it has overlapping nails, studded battens with strap hinges and a cinque-foiled hand plate from the 15th century.

The lower of the windows on the south wall is thought to have been a leper window. Leprosy was a very contagious and unpleasant disease prevalent during the medieval period,

18 Illustration of SS Peter and Paul dated 1848. Note the window in the roof, presumably put in when a balcony for the choir was constructed on the west wall. Also included are drawings of the capitals in the north arcade and the six pieces of glass bearing the words 'Deus ictus' to be found in the Lady Chapel window.

and those suffering from it were not allowed to enter the church. To enable them to watch the services, small windows were strategically placed so that the lepers could view the altar from the outside of the building. Nearby there is also a 14th/15th-century piscina. The porch was rebuilt in the 1880s when the exterior weatherboarding had to be removed in order to evict the bees that had nested there and were

19 Hockley rectory in the 1930s.

20 The tiny parish church of St Mary the Virgin, Hawkwell. Tradition has it that the large oak tree to the right of the picture was planted at the time of the Armada. It was unfortunately cut down in the 1970s.

21 Photograph of Hockley Methodist Church, Rayleigh Road, soon after its construction in 1924.

disturbing the congregation. The money was raised from public subscription, a concert was given at Rochford and the balance was paid by the then rector, the Rev. James Montague.

In the churchyard is the grave of Frances Russel Wallington, wife of one of the rectors, who died in 1848 at 100 years of age. At the eastern end of the churchyard is the final resting place of William Barton, who murdered his wife, a washer woman, in a drunken rage. He might have got away with the murder had not a five-year-old boy called out to him that his wife's body had been found. His nerve cracked and he went to the granary and hung himself. As Barton was a suicide and possible murderer, the rector of the time would not allow him to be interred in consecrated ground. He was therefore buried just outside, in the hedge. To the west of the main door is an area where no gravestones have ever been placed and tradition has it that this is the site of a mass burial for victims of the Great Plague of 1665. As with Hockley, however, there is no historical proof that the plague was present in the Hawkwell area.

Non-conformity came to Hockley in 1881 when preachers from the Southend Wesley Methodist Circuit visited Hockley and preached in the Spa Pump room. The congregation went on to meet in a small hut on Main Road which they rented from the parish church of SS Peter and Paul. Having outgrown the hut, fund raising began and on 1 July 1883 a wooden building with a gallery was opened and Hockley had its own Methodist church. It soon became the centre of communal activity and various groups met there, including the British Women's Total Abstinence Union. In due course further land was purchased for £37 on which to build a new hall at the rear of the chapel. Unfortunately, when the ground was excavated, it was found that the foundations of the chapel were unsafe and the building had to be pulled down. Plans for a new chapel were agreed and the brick building opened on 15 August 1906 at a cost of £958. By 1924 it was obvious there was a need for additional premises and a new hall was erected at the rear of the church.

On 15 December 1925, 16 men and women met in Hockley's schoolroom to make a formal resolution to establish 'worship in the congregational tradition', and the Hockley and Hawkwell United Reformed Church was born. Services were held in the Public Hall until the church opened its own premises, on land donated by a Mr. Read, on Easter Sunday 1929. The first minister was Mr. E.J. Ford, a former missionary in Argentina. In 1930-32 a successful fund-raising campaign enabled them to build the much needed back hall.

A map of 1873 shows the Spa Pump Room in use as a Baptist chapel. However, it was not until 1926, following a camp mission from Clarence Road Baptist Church, Southend, that the area got its first Baptist church in Rectory Road, Hawkwell.

During the early years of this century Hullbridge had a Mission Hall along Ferry Road and it is here that the Salvation Army gave regular monthly services. The Mission Hall had been donated by Miss Crawford of Fambridge Hall, and as a special summer treat Hullbridge children were taken down the river by boat to her home. Eventually the hall had to be demolished when an elm tree fell on it and a new church was opened in 1938 by the Congregational Union. Attached to the church was a hall which could be hired for social events, on condition that there were two of the church elders in attendance. A Mission to Children caravan also made regular fortnightly visits to the village throughout the year.

Perhaps the most unusual form of nonconformity in the area was the sect known as the Peculiar People, who in 1894 opened a chapel in Greensward Lane, Hockley. Started in Rochford in 1855 by James Banyard, a former Wesleyan preacher, they were first

22 Hockley Methodist Church and Rayleigh Road.

23 The opening of the Hockley and Hawkwell United Reformed Church in 1929.

known as Banyardites and the New Lights. They changed their name, inspired by the biblical text from Peter II, 9, 'But ye are a chosen generation, a royal priesthood, an holy nation, a peculiar people.' The used of the word 'peculiar' has changed over the years and at that time was used to specify something special. Local opinion towards them changed when they refused to accept medical aid for themselves and their children. Many were indicted for neglect and served periods of imprisonment. The history of the movement was troubled and eventually there was a split between those members who retained the old beliefs and those who saw the need to change with the times. Twenty years ago the movement changed its name to the Union of Evangelical Churches and the little chapel on Greensward Lane continues today with its very modern congregation.

Chapter Three

Witchcraft and Superstition

THE WITCHCRAFT STATUTES that cover the years 1563-1736 set out clearly the penalties for witchcraft. They list a number of offences including using witchcraft to search for treasure or lost property, injuring people or property, causing the death of a human being, taking dead bodies out of the grave or provoking a person to unlawful love. Punishment, depending upon the severity of the offence, could range from one year's imprisonment to death.

Offences are recorded in the Archdeacon's Rolls at Ingatestone since witchcraft affected men's souls and was therefore the responsibility of the church courts. To protect themselves against the power of witchcraft, people placed inside their boots a piece of paper on which the Lord's Prayer had been written.

Although the nearby village of Canewdon has long been acknowledged as the 'witch capital' of south-east Essex, Hockley also had its share of witches. The first witch we hear of was in 1577 when it was reported that Thomas Barker, a surgeon of Gestingthorpe, together with John Fox, a Hockley labourer, had invoked an evil spirit with the intention of gaining large sums of money. Barker, presumably because of his station in life, was discharged whilst Fox was found guilty. We do not know his sentence, but it was probably one year's imprisonment.

In 1600 Mary Hallinton was extremely lucky when she was brought to the manorial court charged that 'by her evil tongue she bewitched and dismissed [killed] horse, sheep and cattle'. Had she been found guilty then she too would have been referred to the church courts and could have been incarcerated for a year.

We know the fate of John Crushe who in 1642 was accused of sacrificing a lamb to the devil. If he had been found guilty then he would have been executed for conjuring evil spirits.

Tradition has it that witches ride broomsticks. However, in the 19th century a Rochford witch was said to have been seen sailing in a pudding basin on the river Crouch near South Fambridge!

In 1860 Nelly Button, of Hockley, was reputed to have the power to curse those who crossed her. It was said that a young girl refused to bring her some tailoring and as a result Nelly cursed her. The girl went rigid, completely unable to move and the doctors could do nothing to bring her round. However, after a few days the witch whispered in her ear and she recovered. A man who offended her found his concertina playing all night, and a woman's dumplings flew up the chimney! Another victim was the blacksmith who refused to mend her cooking pot. For a week he couldn't sleep for the loud noises that came from his empty forge at night and his wife's cooking pots would not stay on the stove top. The smith, however, knowing that witches cannot cross iron, hid iron items in the hedge around Nelly's cottage only leaving one gap that led straight to Folly Woods. Within a few days she was gone, never to be seen again. Maybe she was a relative of the Annie Button referred to in the section on education—they certainly both appear to have shared the same anti-social tendencies.

Another well known character was Mother Fawkes, who lived near Pulpits Farm in Greensward Lane, Hockley. She would make cows give tainted milk and pigs go off their feed unless she was given an odd loaf of bread or a piece of meat by the farmer. She apparently lived very well by this method of extortion.

Not all witches are female. George Pickingill of Canewdon, who died in about 1909, and Cunning Murrel of Hadleigh are two of the best documented witches in Essex. Although they operated from outside our area it is believed that Pickingill was born in Hockley around 1818, and Murrel had family connections with the village. It was a Murrel who bought the old workhouse next to the church, and after whom Murrel's Lane is named. Elderly Hullbridge residents may still remember Barney the Witch Doctor who lived in Ferry Road and made a formula for restoring hair!

Both Hockley and Hawkwell have stories to tell of a huge black dog with fiery eyes that pads around the village in the dead of night. To see it means a year's bad luck. There are also reports of a ghostly coach and horses passing Hockley church at midnight on Christmas Eve.

In the 1860s people came from far and wide to hear the 'shrieking boy' in Hockley Woods. The disembodied voice claimed that he had been murdered by his mother and his body had been hidden. However, investigation showed that this apparition was nothing more than an owl.

Old superstitions die hard and for many years parents visited Hockley Woods with their crippled children in order to pass them through the split trunk of a tree. These desperate people believed that the deformed tree would take on the crippling disabilities of their children, leaving them straight and strong.

With no doctor to consult during illness people had no alternative but to take the advice of the local wise man or woman for relief. The wet and marshy lands of the Hockley and

24 View of Hockley Woods, *c.*1910.

Hawkwell area were ideal breeding grounds for the mosquito. As a result bouts of 'the ague' (what we would nowadays call malaria) were frequent. In 1803 the local remedy for the ague was to combine 300 grams of snake root, 40 grams of wormwood and a ½ pint of red wine in a bottle and shake well. The medicine was then to be taken in four equal quantities (eight for a child) first thing in the morning and before going to bed, until the attack subsided. The instruction to shake the bottle well before taking it has a remarkably modern ring. Mrs. Print, a pedlar woman, had a better way of treating the ague. She advocated mixing 13d. worth of coal dust with a quarter of gin, drinking the lot in one go and retiring straight to bed!

Bad coughs were treated with stomach plasters. To make a plaster it was necessary to take an ounce each of beeswax, Burgundy, pitch and rosin. The ingredients had then to be melted together in a pipkin and ¾ ounce of common turpentine and ½ ounce of oil of mace added. The resultant paste was then spread on a piece of sheep's leather over which was grated some nutmeg and, whilst still warm, the whole unpleasant mess literally placed on the patient's stomach.

Consumption, what we nowadays call tuberculosis, was a disease common to all classes and despite the many 'cures' available invariably resulted in the patient's death. In 1817 a medicinal recipe stated that a pound of good honey should be gently boiled in a stewpan. To this was added two large sticks of horseradish scraped and grated. The whole concoction was then to be boiled for five minutes, stirring all the time. The patient was to be given two or three tablespoonfuls a day according to their strength.

The following recipe was an infallible cure for the bite of a mad dog:

> Take one ounce of best Dragons Blood [a herb]; of Spanish Brown [also a herb] one ounce and a half; of box leaves, dried and pounded and sifted through a fine sieve, five ounces. Mix together and take in the following manner: To a man or woman, in the morning rising, one large table spoon in a little gruel, white wine, whey or warm milk. To children in proportion. No food for three hours after taking.

The recipe could also be given to a horse or cow, two spoonfuls in warm water or mixed in butter; to a hog one spoonful and a half and to a dog, one spoonful. Whether the patient were human or animal, the medicine should be taken for three mornings in succession as soon as possible after being bitten.

Bee stings were treated with the application of honey and sore eyes were guaranteed to respond if bathed in the first rain that fell in June.

Charms were also sought against various diseases and afflictions. To guard against rheumatism an eel skin garter should be worn. A snake skin worn inside a hat was guaranteed to guard against headaches and taking a piece of sugar soaked in flounder's blood was a sure remedy against whooping cough. If you suffered from cramp then a bag of camphor was to be worn below the knees.

Chapter Four

The Woods of Hockley and Hawkwell

DESPITE THE ENCROACHMENT of agriculture and development, Hockley and Hawkwell have been fortunate in retaining a large number of ancient woods. They include Hockley Woods, Blounts Wood, Folly Wood, Betts Wood, Crabtree Wood, Plumberow Wood, Marylands Wood, Hockley Hall Wood, Hockley Hall Wood South and just on the Hawkwell border, Gusted Hall Wood and Potash Wood.

It is difficult to calculate the extent of woodland in early times. The Domesday Survey tells us that the four major manors in the Hockley/Hawkwell area had 88 pigs between them. Woodland was important, as it was usual in those days to turn the pigs out into the woods in the autumn to feed on the acorns, a practice known as pannage. It is estimated that 10 pigs require 130 acres, which would suggest that the manors of Hockley and Hawkwell had access to approximately 1,300 acres of woodland.

The woods were an important source of fuel and building material for local people. They were carefully managed; the majority of trees were coppiced, that is, cut down to the ground every 10 to 20 years in rotation. The new growth that sprouted from the 'stool' had many

25 Structure of a timber-framed house in the 16th century.

different uses, but was particularly used for fuel, and charcoal. 'Timber' trees were permitted to grow tall and straight for logs and building materials, and it was from Hockley Woods that the foundation piles for Southend Pier were taken. Some trees were pollarded, their branches being cut some 8-10 ft. up the trunk in a similar manner to coppicing, and the new shoots were used for cattle food. Pollards are often found on ancient boundaries and there are a number along footpath 13 to the west of Plumberow Mount. It is pleasing that in several of our local woods coppicing has been reintroduced, thereby increasing the local floral and fauna. It has been calculated that it took 173 trees to build the Old House in South Street, Rochford, and there would have been many such buildings in the Rochford Hundred.

By the middle ages woodland ownership was well defined and carefully guarded. However, not all the manors had woods close by, as was the case with Beaches Manor, Rawreth, which owned woodland in what we today collectively call Hockley Woods. Such ownership is known by the technical term 'exclave'.

26 An early photograph of The Old House, South Street, Rochford, a timber-framed building dating back to the 13th century. Restored in the 1970s, it is now the offices of Rochford District Council.

The oldest record of woodland in the area is at Plumberow and dates from 1237 when there is mention of a wood called Langelegh. A survey of 1264 refers to Kyng Welle Wode, Berisgrove and Smalethornegrove. By the time the map of 1576 was drawn, Plumberow had changed considerably. Kangle Wood is presumably the Kyngwellewode referred to earlier, but there was also a substantial wood called Spurges. It is possible that Plumberow Manor had fallen on hard times because it had changed from arable to predominantly pasture, which is less labour intensive. The new agricultural practice had not been sufficient to prevent the hedges from expanding and forming strip woodland and groves. The hedgerows were a valuable asset. The survey stated that the rent from the farm was £50 per annum, while the total value of the standing timber and wood on the estate was £564 per annum. The timber and wood standing in the hedges and groves, excluding the two major woods, were worth no less than £261 alone! The only wood left today is Plumberow Wood, which was originally described as 'one Grove or Hedge rowe called Plomborowe Hill Hedgerowe'. It was then about twice the length of the present wood, but only 90 yards wide, less than half its width today. Plumberow Mount is to the south of the wood; the 1576 map shows a structure on top of it, perhaps a summer house like the one that was built on it in the early years of the 20th century.

The survey of 1687 shows the lands held by the manor of Hockley. Hockley Hall Wood, which has a fine collection of wood banks, has altered very little since that time. Hockley Hall Wood South lies to the south of the railway line, and is in fact a small part of Hockley Hall Wood which was cut in two when the railway was built. The map does not include Crabtree Wood, which abuts it.

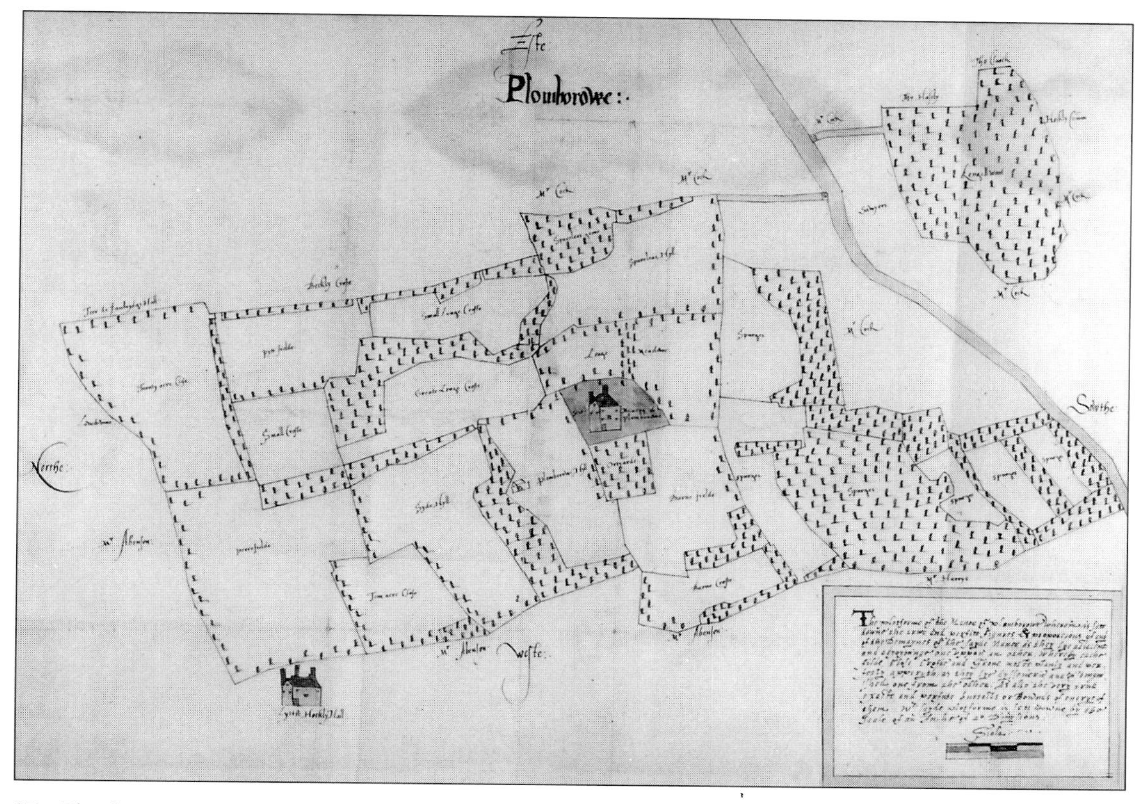

27 Plumberow map of 1576. North is to the left. The large road to the right of the page is the present Greensward Lane. Although Marylands Wood did not belong to the estate, it is shown just above the left-hand corner of the text. (Reproduced by permission of the British Library.)

Although not documented, it is obvious that Marylands Wood has a very long history as some of the coppice stools are of an enormous size. Unfortunately the large natural pond in the wood, once on the edge of Hockley Common, is suffering from the changes to the water table that have taken place in recent years and is slowly drying up. The pond was obviously much deeper earlier this century as elderly Hockley residents can remember fishing and swimming in it as children. Today's children still enjoy fishing in its murky water for newts and tadpoles. To the south of the pond there is an ancient woodbank, beyond which is secondary woodland that has grown since the coming of the railway when a field was cut in two. A local conservation group has resumed coppicing in the wood thanks to the support of the local landowner.

The small woods of Blounts, also cut in two by the railway, Folly and Betts all have long histories, and Betts Wood is now being cared for by the children of nearby Hockley Primary School.

There are two theories about the origin of the name of Potash Wood, just over the Hawkwell border. Chapman and André's map of 1777 gives the name as Puttocks Wood, a puttock being a buzzard or kite. Alternatively, it could refer to the production of potash which was an important woodland industry in the past. Potash was made in great quantities in the 19th century and had many uses: particularly as a fertiliser, for bleaching linen, in dying, and

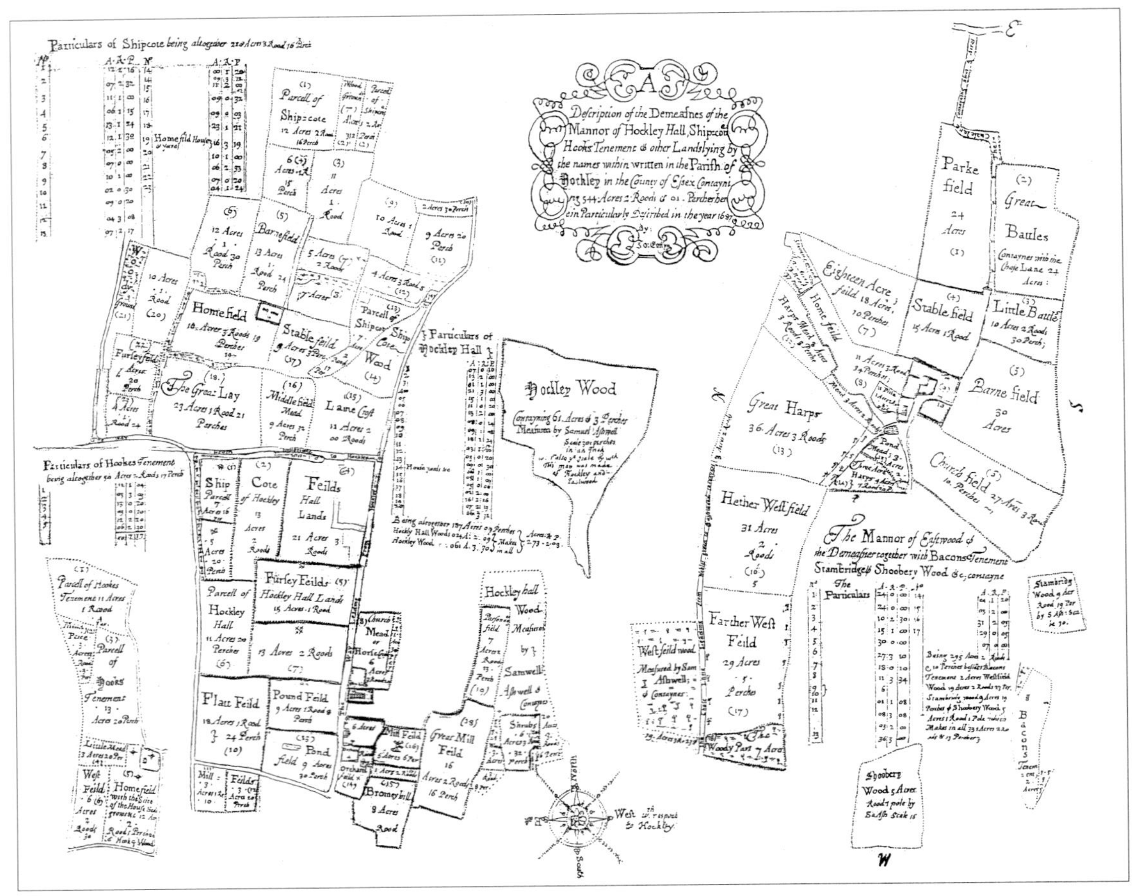

28 Survey of 1687 showing lands held by Hockley manor. The map on the right refers to land held at Eastwood, Stambridge and Shoebury. Hockley Woods are in the centre, and the Hockley estate is shown on the left. Note the tiny drawings of Hockley church and the windmill. (Reproduced by permission of the Master and Fellows of Wadham College, Oxford.)

in the manufacture of glass, Woodash, the main ingredient, was collected from local people, who were paid 5d. a bushel. To make potash the ashes were put in tubs with perforated bottoms and water was poured over them. The water, saturated with salts, filtered through to another container called a lye-letch. Wheat, oat or barley straw were then soaked in the water. The straw was dried and burned on the hearth, taking care only to let it smoulder. The resultant ash was mixed with water and the process repeated again and again before the final product was ready for market. The whole process consumed an enormous amount of wood, 1,300 tons of dry oak and 1,800 tons of green oak being required to extract one ton of potash.

Gusted Hall Wood is first mentioned in 1450 as Gristedwode and to the north includes a strip of secondary woodland taken in about 100 years ago from the now vanished Hawkwell Lower Common.

Hockley Woods are without a doubt the best known in the area, and comprise Beaches Wood, Great Hawkwell Wood, Parsons Snipe (which once belong to Hawkwell church), Great Bull Wood, Little Bull Wood, Whitbread Wood, Winks Wood and Hawkwell Wood.

The parish boundary between Hawkwell and Hockley passes through the middle following an ancient woodbank. Despite encroachment by agriculture and development, the woods have changed little since the map of 1687. Prior to the reformation Great Bull Wood, named it is believed after *The Bull Inn*, belonged to Hockley manor and to the nuns at Barking Abbey. After the reformation Beaches Wood was acquired by Sion College, London and Hawkwell Wood became the property of Christ's College, Cambridge.

Although in private hands, by the beginning of the 20th-century Hockley Woods had been open to the public for some years and became a popular place to visit for a day's outing. In April 1928 a local magazine, 'The Hockley News', reported on the Easter holiday, telling of the flood of visitors arriving every few minutes from London by train, the large number of cars and motor cycles on the roads and how all the buses to Hockley were full. As the woods were rather muddy, some shoeblacks did a roaring trade when they set up a stand in the late afternoon and long queues formed for visitors to have their shoes cleaned before returning home. No doubt a few of the visitors stayed late to hear the nightingales, for which the woods were famous. Unfortunately the day was not without incident, for two cars collided on the High Road by the water fountain.

The Horslin family opened a tea garden with a large marque and smaller pavilions where visitors could sit and take their refreshments at ease. Donkey rides on the strangely named 'Jerusalem donkeys', who were kept in a field next to the school, were a popular attraction. Thatched summer houses were built in the woods and bowls and tennis were available.

29 The Old Nursery, once on the High Road, Hockley. With no other building material to hand, and brick and slate being too expensive for the ordinary labourer, wood and thatch were used extensively throughout the area for building.

30 *Above.* Entrance to Bull Woods, Hockley.

31 *Above right.* The horse trough and water fountain in Hockley Woods.

32 *Right.* A charabanc outing to Hockley photographed outside the *Bull Inn*, 1914. The gentleman standing to the front of the picture wearing a bowler hat is the licensee, Mr. Bowen.

However, while visitors could enjoy the pleasures of the woods, they were still a place of employment for many local people. Charcoal burners were to be seen sitting patiently by their great smoking stacks and firewood was collected and sent in great bundles to London. At Christmas time gypsies came to cut holly to sell and in the autumn local children collected chestnuts for which they were paid 6d a bag.

The horse trough and drinking fountain at the entrance to Hockley Woods is a fairly recent addition. It was originally installed in the Market Square, Rochford, to commemorate the coronation of Edward VII, and moved to its present position when the square was replanned. At the time of writing consideration is being given to returning it to its original home.

In 1930 the Rochford Rural Council purchased the woods at a cost of £2,800, thereby preserving them for the future enjoyment of visitors.

THE CORONATION OF
EDWARD VII

33 The Horslin family who ran the Hockley Tea Gardens, 1915.

34 Entrance to Hockley Tea Gardens, 1915.

35 Entrance to the Hockley Tea Gardens, 1915. Note the Hockley Public Hall in the background.

36 Hockley Tea Gardens, 1915.

37 *Above left.* Happy visitors taking their ease in the Hockley Tea Gardens. The elderly lady is in a wicker Bath chair.

38 *Left.* Hockley Tea Gardens. Note the see-saw made out of a plank of wood and a tree trunk.

39 *Above.* The Jerusalem Donkeys.

40 *Right.* 'Dobber' Shelley, the local thatcher, working on the summerhouses in Hockley Woods.

41 One of the hundreds of postcards produced to sell to the visitors who came to Hockley to enjoy the woods and the countryside.

42 A charcoal burner.

43 Woodland dwellers outside their cottage. To the right of the picture are bundles of firewood ready to be sold locally and sent as far afield as London.

44 Feeding the chickens in Hockley Woods.

Chapter Five

Poverty and Despair

DESPITE THE IMPROVEMENTS in farming practices in the 18th century, south-east Essex remained a sparsely populated and poor agricultural area. In 1831 the population of the whole of Rochford Hundred was only 777 people. The Report of the Royal Commission on the Poor Law for 1834 states that an agricultural labourer with a wife and four children between the ages of five and 14 years, could expect to earn only £40 per year. This did not take into account the fact that labourers were paid by the day and, if the weather was bad, there was no work and therefore no pay. In the summer women and children could earn 6-10d. per day on the land from hoeing, weeding, haymaking, dropping and picking potatoes, but there was very little winter work, apart perhaps from collecting stones off the fields. There was therefore little, if any, money to be put aside for a 'rainy day'. The same report gives the labourer's diet as principally bread, potatoes, tea and occasionally a little meat and beer. Maybe once a week there would be cheese to eat with the potatoes.

In the 1870s people continued to leave the area because of bad farming conditions, the fall in the price of wheat, the high tithe rate and the lack of clean drinking water. Things were so bad that by 1871 it was said that only old people and fools were left in the villages of Rochford Hundred. However, a large number of Scottish farmers moved into the area, finding it preferable to the conditions they had left behind them.

The residents of Hockley and Hawkwell had access to three charities in their need, two of which are still in operation. In the 16th century a parcel of land on the Plumberow Estate had been left to the parishes of Hockley and Rayleigh, the rent from which was to provide for the local poor. In 1795 the land was exchanged for some on the Southend Road which became known as the Poores Land. Following the enclosure of Hockley's common, this land served Hockley as its open space, becoming known in later years as Spa Meadow. Hawkwell's charity, the Sudbury's Charity, dates from 1615, when Robert Sudbury left money to purchase a parcel of land, the rents to be bestowed on 'fatherless children in Eastwood, Hockley and Hawkwell by even and equal portions, except all bastards and idle persons'. Unfortunately Joslyn's Charity, dating back to 1604 and administered by the churchwardens and minister of Prittlewell, which was intended to purchase wood, provide for houses and relieve the necessities of the poor, aged and distressed, no longer exists.

Before the establishment of the Welfare State the frail, poor, elderly and vulnerable had no alternative but to seek aid from the 'parish' or to accept charity. At Hockley the elderly of the village with no family to care for them were either admitted to the almshouse, once on Drover's Hill, or the workhouse near the tollgate at the junction of Spa Road with Southend Road. No evidence of either building remains, although one of the fields in the vicinity of Whitbreads appears as 'the paupers

45 Harry Cottis in his trap on the Spa Meadow, 1920.

46 Flower Show, Spa Meadow.

field' on maps well into the last century. In 1811 both buildings were sold for the sum of £223 and the money was used to build a new workhouse next to the church. This in turn was sold in 1843 to a Mr. Murrel, Hoyman of Hockley, for £202 and the money was transferred to the new Rochford Union Workhouse, later to become Rochford Hospital. Hawkwell's parish workhouse, once along Ironwell Lane, was also sold and the proceeds passed to the Union workhouse at Rochford.

Conditions in the Union workhouse were stark and the residents were expected to work if they were in a physical condition to do so. The working day started at 6 a.m. with bedtime at 9 p.m. (8 p.m. in the winter). The sexes were segregated and the paupers lived in virtual isolation, not being permitted visitors nor allowed outside the walls of the complex.

The less vulnerable poor were not admitted to the workhouse, but received a weekly dole which was paid out to them at the *Spa Hotel*. They were, however, expected to earn their money and in 1855 the men who were sent to work on the railway earned just enough bread for themselves and their families for each of the days they worked.

In 1853 we learn of the sad story of Henry Stowers of Hockley who was on the verge of giving up his work in order to care for his wife, who was 'nearly a lunatic', and his five children. Desperate to find someone to help look after her, but unable to pay for such assistance from his 12s. 0d. a week wages, he applied to the Board of Guardians at the Rochford Union for financial assistance. The Board decided to take a couple of the children into the workhouse which they believed would release enough income to enable the father to pay for a nurse!

Orphaned children were also the responsibility of the Rochford Union and a home for them was built in Bullwood Approach, now Southend Cottages. Having received their education locally they were put out to work, the boys as apprentices, the girls into service. The Board of Guardian minutes of 1864 proudly boast that 'none of these children have

47 Hawkwell Workhouse, once in Ironwell Lane, Hawkwell, and demolished in the 1960s.

48 The Rochford Union Workhouse, 1900, later to become Rochford Hospital.

49 Prittlewell Pesthouse, once on the east side of Eastwood Lane. It was erected in the 18th century and demolished in 1914.

been returned'. Life was not all drudgery and hard work, as the reply to a letter from the proprietor of the *Ship Hotel*, Southend on Sea proves. In it the Board of Guardians grant permission for him to take the children out for a treat.

The workhouse also served as a hospital but, in the case of an infectious disease such as cholera, patients were sent to the isolation hospital or 'pest house' in Prittlewell. In 1866 there was a particularly bad outbreak of cholera at Rochford which lasted for four weeks.

The depression of the 1920/30s did not pass by the Hockley and Hawkwell area. One elderly resident remembers well the homeless man who lived in an old threshing machine on Hawkwell Common and another who lived in a farm stable. After the First World War, when the tractor became the norm and farm horses disappeared from the land, Tommy Horslin, the village blacksmith, found himself out of work. He could not adapt to mechanisation and so took a job in Runwell, some eight miles away, walking there and back each day. When that job finished, he went to work even further afield in Maldon, cycling 20 miles each way.

There are always those who will not be helped. For instance, a newspaper article of January 1931 tells of Joseph Woodward, a 71-year-old hermit who was found dead huddled against the half open door of the wooden hut in which he lived near Hockley Woods. Beside

50 Hockley's smithy, where Tommy Horslin worked until the coming of mechanisation after the First World War made him redundant.

him was the quarter of a pound of meat and a loaf of bread he had just bought. Apparently he had lived the life of a hermit for at least 30 years and earned what living he could from doing odd jobs.

In 1936 William and Alice Stredder of Hillcrest Terrace, Hockley were charged with neglecting their six children. Although it had to be admitted that the family lived in filthy surroundings, the husband's defence was that, having heard there was work at Dagenham, he had cycled there to secure it. Having got the job he stayed at Dagenham all week, cycling home at the weekend. He wrote to his wife to inform her of the situation, but she did not read the letter and, thinking he had left her, abandoned the children. The matter came before the court who sent her to prison for three months so that she could receive relief from worry and regain her strength!

Chapter Six

Educating the Masses

AN INQUISITION by the London Board of Education, dated 1839, gives us an insight into the education accessible to the labouring classes in Hockley in the early 19th century. From 1828-1839 the only education available to this small agricultural community was a Sunday School which operated from a cottage near the church. 20 boys and 25 girls attended and the furthest any child had to walk was two miles.

Following a successful bid to the National Society of the Church of England, a national school was built on the site of the old vicarage next to the church. The accommodation consisted of two rooms, one 20 ft. by 15 ft. to accommodate 50 boys, and the other 21 ft. by 16 ft. for 72 girls and infants. The cost of the school, plus the teacher's house, amounted to £540, of which £345 was raised by public subscription locally and the balance from the Society and the government. There was only one school mistress who was paid £35 a year and was assisted by monitors. The children paid 1d. or 2d. per week to attend according to their parents' means, and many still had to walk several miles a day to get to and from school.

51 Church Lane, Hockley. The old school is on the right, just before the church.

52 The old school house, Hockley, after it had been turned into a private dwelling in the 1950s.

Education was basic: reading, writing, the homilies of the Church of England, geography, needlework, the Bible, the Book of Common Prayer and the Thirty-nine Articles of Religion. An inspector in 1857 reported only 34 children present, who were being taught by a 20-year-old teacher. He also stated that the children were mostly very young, instruction was elementary and the accommodation 'fair'.

For the wealthier children in the community, still too young to go away to school, there was a Dame School at Rayleigh.

In May 1882 the school transferred to the Hockley School Board and in 1903 moved to new premises on the Main Road, with a house next door for the headmaster. There the school stayed until the 1970s when it moved to its current location on Betts Farm, leaving the old building to be converted to an information technology centre. With the increase in population during the 1950s and '60s it became obvious that a further infant/junior school was necessary, and Plumberow School was opened in Hamilton Gardens.

For a short time in the 1930s the Rev. Gardner at Hockley ran a school at the vicarage for a small number of privileged young 'gentlemen'. Amongst their number was a Burmese prince who, with his sports car and wealth, swept one of the local girls off her feet and into trouble. She accompanied him back to Burma, but sadly the relationship did not last.

Hullbridge gained its own school in 1903. The situation prior to that date is unclear. A map of 1873 shows an infants school in Ferry Road, which perhaps indicates that it was the older children from Hullbridge who had to make the two-mile walk to Hockley school for their education. The school at Hullbridge was smaller than the one at Hockley; with the addition of the master's house it cost £65 11s. 0d., including furniture, and £50 for the site. Only three years later a survey of the premises found that substantial improvements were needed, in particular sanitation, lighting, ventilation and the supply of drinking water.

In 1903 there is the first reference to a child being admitted to the school from across the river Crouch at Woodham Ferrers. The children were ferried across the river at high tide, but when the tide was out they had to

53 The new Hockley School, with the teacher's house next door, 1917. Note the thatched barn to the far left.

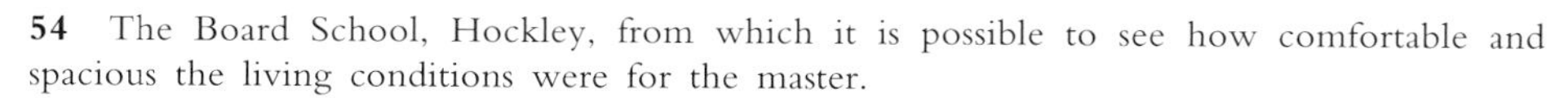

54 The Board School, Hockley, from which it is possible to see how comfortable and spacious the living conditions were for the master.

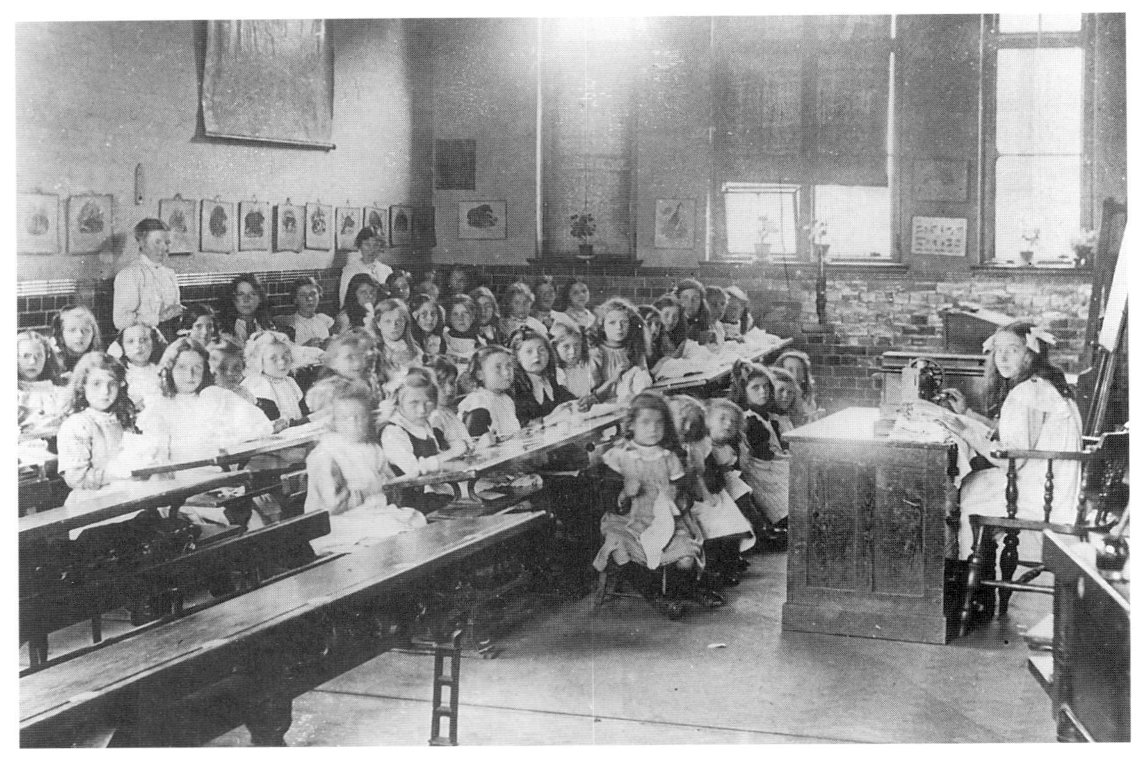

55 A sewing lesson at Hockley School, 1901.

56 The pupils of Hockley School, 1921.

57 The pupils of the Rev. Gardner's school for young gentlemen, 1922. The Burmese prince is second from the left, front row.

make the perilous journey across the causeway by horse and cart. There were many complaints that the ferry, only a rowing boat, was frequently late and that it was dangerously overcrowded, the children having to sit on each other's laps. Things got so bad that in 1907 the school's management committee wrote to the owner asking that, for safety's sake, no more than eight children be carried at any one time.

Not only did the children from across the river have a difficult journey, but many had long, lonely walks to school in all weathers. In 1911 cocoa was provided to augment their food at a charge of ls. 2d. per week per child. It was also suggested that the cloakrooms should be heated so that the children could dry their clothes.

All the local schools were encouraged to compete for an attendance shield which Hullbridge held for a record nine months. To ensure punctuality the headmaster, Mr. Snelgar, rang a handbell that could be heard throughout the village.

By 1974 the school had moved to a new site at the other end of the village, leaving the old building for community use.

In 1846 the Rev. Yorke, Rector of Hawkwell, Algernon White of Clements Hall and Samuel Baker of Hawkwell Hall completed a questionnaire for the National Society for the Promotion of Education, in which they stated that there was no school in the parish of Hawkwell and that the children had to travel to Rochford for their education. The questionnaire also noted that Samuel Baker had donated land on the turnpike road on which to erect a school house and master's house and that £100 had been raised by public

58 Children from the north bank of the Crouch crossing the river by trap to attend Hullbridge School.

subscription to build it. As no land had been identified as a playspace, the children could play on the common or the open road, now one of the busiest roads in south-east Essex! As a result of the questionnaire, Hawkwell's school was opened in 1847. Twelve children, described in the school log as 'backward', attended on the first day. In 1878 the school log records that the manners of the children were 'rough'. The girls, in addition to doing their lessons, were expected to sweep the premises at the end of the day. To keep pace with a growing population it was necessary to extend the premises and a gallery was built around the infants room in 1895. In 1897 the log mentions 'many more children come to live in the parish'.

In 1904 the school was again extended by an additional room for infants and juniors, and the gallery was removed. Problems with overcrowding continued and in 1907 children above the age of nine years were sent to Hockley. By 1920 the future of Hawkwell school was in doubt and three years later it closed for six months. It closed again just three years later, this time for several years. Various suggestions were put forward for its use, including a cookery school. However, local residents fought hard to keep it and in 1929 it opened again. By the 1970s it had become obvious that the building was inadequate and it was closed for good and eventually demolished, a new school being erected in the appropriately named Sunny Road.

All three schools shared the same problems: children with long and difficult journeys to make and conflicts with family loyalties. If the mother of the family was unwell and there were other children to be cared for, then it was often expected that the eldest daughter would stay at home and look after them, no matter how long it took for the mother to recover or how much the child's education might suffer. Absences to work on the land, whether it be pea picking, gleaning or helping in the harvest field, were common in an agricultural community. The few pennies earned by the children in the fields were a much welcome addition to a labourer's income. A reference in the Hawkwell log of December 1896 tells of boys being absent to drive birds for a shooting party at Clements Hall.

School could be closed for days or even weeks if the weather turned bad or there was an epidemic of measles, scarlatina or the new 'chicken pox'. Attendance also fell when there was a visit from the Band of Hope, or the fair arrived in Rayleigh.

All three logs tell of older children being admitted to school without having received any education whatsoever, and also of pupils being sent home because they were too filthy to stay in the classroom. There are many references to boys, and girls, being punished for bad behaviour. Hockley's log makes special mention of Annie Button who was punished in April 1885 for insubordination. The master stated that 'in all his experience as a teacher, he had never had so much impudence and stubbornness from any child'. Bad language was a problem then as it is now, for on 3 October 1887 George Hart of Hockley was punished for using 'foul language'. Obviously George's punishment was no deterrent, for on the 21st of the same month four boys were also punished for using filthy language to the girls during the dinner hour. In 1895 the buttons of all the coats in the infants room at Hawkwell school were cut off. The perpetrator of the deed was never discovered! Smoking in school was also a problem over 100 years ago, for in 1896 Fred Barnes was punished for doing just that.

There was also a lighter side to life at school in those early days. Hullbridge had its May Queen and May pole. The children at Hockley were taken on treats to Shoebury Common and Hadleigh Castle in shooting brakes, and in the 1930s there was a visit to London Zoo by train. There was a great deal of excitement on Empire Day and Armistice

59 Hawkwell village centre. The first building on the left is the old school house.

60 & 61 Children at Hawkwell School.

62 The Greensward County Secondary School, Hockley, soon after it was built.

Day with parades and special songs. Hockley had a curious tradition called '1 lb. day' when each child brought in 1 lb. of goods to be sent to the orphanage at Nazareth House, Southend. The 1st May was 'tip hat day' and the 2nd, 'petticoat day', when the boys were allowed to chase the girls and pull their petticoats down! On Oak Apple Day, 29 May, for some strange reason, the children armed themselves with nettles and chased around trying to whip each other with them.

In the majority of cases children left school at 14 years, although in 1886 Sarah Safill of Hawkwell left unexpectedly to go into service at Southend at the early age of thirteen. In 1937 children over eleven years transferred to Rayleigh Secondary School. Those who were particularly gifted could take an examination and go to Southend High School or Clarks College, Southend. As the population increased in the 1960s, Hockley gained its own secondary school in Greensward Lane.

Chapter Seven

Getting Around—By River, Road and Rail

THE HEAVY CLAY SOILS of south-east Essex made transport by the few existing roads difficult and until the coming of the railway the easiest method of transporting man, animals and materials was via the river Crouch. To get to the other side of the river and on to the Chelmsford road, it was possible to ford the river at the bottom of Ferry Road at Hullbridge, as it is today for the not too faint-hearted! In due course a bridge was built. The first reference to it is dated 1549 when John Tyrell, Lord of the Manor of Beeches, bequeathed the sum of £11 0s. 0d. for the making up of the bridge 'for Master Griffith's soul'. Unfortunately we do not know who Master Griffiths was. By 1562 the bridge was once more in a bad state of repair, and despite calls for assistance, no one could be found to take responsibility for it. Things must have improved for in 1594 Sir Thomas Montgomery of Faulkebourne Hall, near Witham, left £20 0s. 0d. in his will for its repair.

63 The River Crouch at the bottom of Ferry Road, Hullbridge, 1920s.

64 The Hullbridge ferry looking back at Hullbridge from the north bank.

By 1645 things had got so bad that the bridge had been replaced by a horse ferry run by the landlord of the then *Anchor Inn*, who charged one penny for a foot passenger, two-pence per horse and the same for a coach. Prices continued to rise and in 1766 the cost of transporting a man or horse had increased to 6d. Not all ferrymen were honest, however, and there are constant references in the Chelmsford Assizes to ferrymen defrauding their passengers. John Tinley in particular appears five times for overcharging.

It is possible that some kind of plank footbridge spanned the river until at least 1766, for a Quarter Sessions entry of that date refers to the repairing of Hullbridge.

Although the bridge has long gone, a hole in the bed of the river known locally as the 'sump' remains, caused, it is believed, by the continual rush of water through the centre arch of the bridge. The ferry continued until 1948 when Dick Hymas, ferryman for 20 years, ceased operations.

In 1901 Hockley Parish Council, in consultation with the residents of Hullbridge, decided that travel to Chelmsford would be easier if the bridge over the river was reinstated. So began 22 years of discussion. Petitions were taken to the Rochford Rural Council, pamphlets were written and meetings were held with the Woodham Ferrers Bridge Committee. The biggest stumbling block, however, was the apparent inability of the parish council to discover who owned the ferry. Eventually, in 1923, they made the amazing discovery that it belonged to the brewery that owned the *Anchor Inn*—Henry Tucker and Co. of Southend—and whose tenant was still running the ferry service. Eventually, however, it had to be admitted that the cost of constructing a modern bridge in an area of reclaimed marsh would be prohibitive and the idea was dropped.

As the area began to develop, so did the trade on the Crouch. Materials for the large number of houses being built in the area were shipped up the river, in addition to construction

65 Thames barge caught in the frozen river Crouch, 1920s.

66 Dick Hymas, Hullbridge's last ferryman, who retired in 1948 after 20 years' service.

equipment for the railway. To meet the demand, jetties grew up along the river and Hullbridge gained in importance as it is one of the few places on the river Crouch which has direct access to the water. Thames barges were a familiar sight, returning to London laden with agricultural produce and hay for the many horses in the city.

Before the river was as highly embanked as it is today, it was not uncommon for it to freeze over completely. The story is told of Thomas and John Fitch of High Elms, Hullbridge, who during the severe frost of 1795 walked across the frozen river at high tide. In the same year a horse and cart also travelled across safely.

Up until this century, the upkeep of roads remained a problem. Roads were the responsibility of the parish and it was up to the parish surveyor to ensure that landowners maintained their particular part of the highway, which they frequently failed to do. In 1667 Richard Massum of Eastwood was summoned for not clearing his ditch leading from Nobles Green in Eastwood towards Hawkwell, and in 1669 Thomas Binckes of Prittlewell, who farmed at Hockley, was fined £30 for not sending his team to assist with the repair of the highway.

In 1747 road conditions began to improve when the Essex Turnpike Trust extended its metalled road from the *Eagle and Lamb* in Shenfield to Rochford, via Hockley and Hawkwell, and from then on to Leigh. Toll gates were set up at regular intervals along the route, the one at Hockley being located almost opposite the *Spa Hotel*. To pass through the toll gate a charge had to be paid. In 1815 a coach, Berlin, Landau or chariot drawn by six horses cost 2s. 6d. and a stage coach carrying six or more, also drawn by six horses, was 2s. 0d. It was not only carriages or stage coaches which were charged to go through the gate. Farmers also had to pay for their animals at the rate of 3d. to 6d. per score, and a riding horse cost 1d. Although Hawkwell did not have a tollgate, there was one on the

67 The frozen river Crouch in about 1920.

68 Extract from deed of the *Spa Hotel* dated 1843 showing the Hockley turnpike and turnpike cottage. (Reproduced by permission of Allied Domecq Inns.)

69 Hockley's turnpike cottage prior to its demolition in the 1960s. The turnpike cottage had been a well known fish shop.

70 Milestone on Drovers Hill, Hockley.

Hawkwell/Rochford border. Tradition has it that, rather than pay to travel along the turnpike to Rochford, Hawkwell residents bypassed the gates by cutting across country, creating in the process the green lane now known as Ironwell Lane. How true this story is we do not know, but by the time Chapman and André published their county map in 1777, it was important enough to be shown. It is more likely, however, that this was the original road to Rochford which was abandoned when the smoother and quicker turnpike road was built.

In 1836 Alan Bates' 'Directory of Stage Coach Services' lists one coach a day from London to Southend, departing from *The Bull*, Aldgate, via Ilford, Romford, Brentwood, Billericay, Wickford, Rayleigh and Rochford. The coach, owned by J. Tabor and Company, left Southend at 7.45 a.m. to reach London at 1.45 p.m., returning at 2.45 p.m. and arriving at Southend by 8.45 p.m. *The Despatch* as the coach was called, carried 15 people, four inside and 11 outside. Rochford also had another coach from Mondays to Saturdays, owned by J. Thorogood, with a London terminus at the *Blue Boar*, Aldgate.

Milestones were a necessity as maps were scarce and very expensive. Those marked with Roman numerals are considered to be the earliest; the others, giving the distance to Southend, are much later as Leigh was the original destination of the turnpike. At that time Southend was little more than a fishing village at the south end of Prittlewell, whilst Leigh on the other hand was a prosperous port, described by the 18th-century historian, Morant, as 'a pretty little town stocked with lusty seamen'.

Although motor cars were initially few in number, their increased popularity in the early years of the century caused real problems. Not least for the Hockley Parish Council, whose clerk wrote in 1910 to Essex County Council drawing attention to 'the danger to life through motor cars travelling on the Main Road near Hockley House'. A 'danger signal'

71 Mr. and Mrs. Inifer Potter and family, who owned a grocery shop in Hockley, *c.*1916.

72 Mr. and Mrs. Inifer Potter, proudly displaying their new automobile, early 1920s.

73 Lark's Garage in the centre of Hockley.

74 The interior of Hockley Motors.

75 Hockley Motors, one of the many garages that grew up in the area in the 1920s/30s.

76 For those brave enough, it was possible to ford the river at Hullbridge in a motorcar. However, not everyone who tried was successful!

on the corner of Fountain Lane was called for in February 1912, and a petition submitted to the county council in 1922 asking for action to be taken following the collision between a horse and cart and a car. In 1923 two motor cars got stuck for two days in the trenches that were being dug to bring gas to the village. In the same year the chairman of the parish council was nearly run over when making an official visit to inspect the dangerous Folly Lane junction with Alderman's Hill, which had been the subject of numerous complaints.

The very fact that the area was basically agricultural could cause unexpected problems for the unwary driver. In 1899 Mr Caplin of Bartons Farm on the Lower Road, Hockley, was accused by the parish council of causing an obstruction by driving and feeding his cows on the highway. A large and no doubt smelly mound of manure left on the roadside at Bull Lane, Hockley, was also the subject of complaint and the parish clerk was asked to take necessary action to have it removed. Then, as now, parking on the footway was a common problem, although in November 1911 the offenders were carts and not cars!

In 1840 the Eastern Counties Railway reached Brentwood from Shoreditch. Realising the potential for further traffic, it then opened a station at Shenfield where stagecoach travellers could be picked up. Bradshaw's *Railway Guide* for 1849 lists two trains a day in each direction, but on Sunday there were three 'up' and four 'down'. The venture was not a success and in 1850 it closed. Various other plans were suggested for bringing the railway to Hockley, including one via Ingatestone!

77 Even bad weather did not stop Mr. Inifer Potter from delivering provisions to his customers. Here he is being pulled on a sledge by Mini the piebald pony, 1912-13.

78 Mini the piebald pony and Mr. Inifer Potter outside the shop in central Hockley, 1912-13.

79 Mr. Inifer Potter in his pony and trap, 1912.

80 Digging out the Hockley cutting by hand, pre-1886.

However, in 1886 the first sod was cut and the line from Shenfield to Wickford was started. In 1889 the single track finally reached Southend and was opened to great jubilation on 1 October. Such was the excitement that, as we know from the Hockley School log book, a number of children played truant so that they could watch the first train pass through and join in the celebrations.

Both Hockley and Hawkwell had sidings; Hawkwell's was located where the two railwaymen's cottages are in Rectory Road. Built specifically to serve the agricultural community, it was not a success and was discontinued in 1900.

Although two cottages and a substantial house were built for railway staff along Station Approach, Hockley, the station was too small to warrant a station master and Rochford assumed responsibility for its working. The business of the line in those early days was local working: moving bricks, coal, fish and the local population. There was only one train a day between Liverpool Street and Southend, which left Southend at 1.45 p.m. and reached Liverpool Street at 3.10 p.m.

In the summer of 1891 the first business train left Southend at 8.45 a.m. destined to reach Liverpool Street at 9.50 a.m. It left Liverpool Street that evening at 5.25 p.m to return to Southend at 6.30 p.m. This was no ordinary train and could only have been used by top management, as ordinary workers would have started work long before it even set out on its journey. The age of the commuter had begun.

Business was booming and in 1896 the track was doubled from Prittlewell to Rochford, but the section between Rochford and Wickford had to wait until 1901 before it received the same treatment. By 1911 it took 52 minutes and 25 seconds to travel from Southend to Liverpool Street and for a while restaurant cars with attentive waiters and waitresses were provided on some of the services.

As a result of the Railway Act of 1921 the Great Eastern Railway became part of the London and North Eastern Railway, gaining for itself the affectionate title of the 'Late and Never Early Railway' (LNER). The age of steam was not to last and in 1956 electric trains were running through Hockley and Hawkwell.

81 View of Hockley Station and the houses built for railway staff.

82 Hockley station, 1908. Note the signal box on the left and the roof over the walkway.

Chapter Eight

Hockley Spa

BY THE EARLY 1840s visits to the seaside for the sake of one's health had become the fashion. In 1841 a Dr. A.B. Granville undertook a tour of the south coast to evaluate the health-giving benefits of the Isle of Wight, Broadstairs and Ramsgate. He was disappointed in what he found and terminated his journey at Dover leaving, as he put it, 'the cockneyfied watering-places of the Isle of Thanet to their own well and familiarly known merits'. Having heard from a friend of Southend's reputation, he travelled there, taking in as he did so Hockley and its new spa. However, he did have his doubts about the journey for, as he put it,

> Essex is a county with a bad name and when I heard of a spa being about to be established in that part of it which, like a peninsula, lies between the river Crouch and its marshes to the north and the Thames and its lowlands to the south, I turned up my nose at the idea.

He was, however, pleasantly surprised, for what he found were pretty villages, beautiful views and pure air.

Mineral springs are not uncommon on London clay and have been recorded at Woodham Ferrers, Ilford (St Chad's Well), South Benfleet and Hawkwell (Ironwell Lane). The medicinal properties of Hockley's mineral well were 'discovered' in the late 1830s by a Mr. and Mrs. Clay. They had dug a well to supply their new villa with water, but at the time were unaware of any of its health-giving properties. The Clays had recently moved from Cheltenham to Hockley in the hope that the country air would relieve Mrs. Clay's asthma and persistent cough. She noted that when she left Hockley for even short periods her health problems returned and she eventually came to the conclusion that it was the well water that held the secret to her improved health. Said to be 10 ft. deep, the well, it was claimed, never ran dry even in the hottest weather and never froze in the coldest.

The water, which was bubbly and tasted slightly acidic, was analysed and found to contain common salt, bicarbonate of lime, sulphate of magnesia and sulphate of lime, what we today would call Epsom salts. Having lived at Cheltenham, itself a spa, Mrs. Clay saw the potential for her well and set up her own spa from her house, now renamed Hockley Spa Lodge. Claims were made that the water could help disorders of the kidney, stomach complaints and even rickets. To gain the full benefit visitors had to drink one and a half pints of the water, four times a day, straight from the well. The water did have some alarming properties. It was noted that lead and iron corroded rapidly when they came into contact with it!

It was not long before the locally famous spa caught the attention of big business. In 1843 a London solicitor by the not inappropriate name of Fawcett of Cripplegate, London, took over the business and, having engaged the services of well known architect James Lockyer, erected a purpose-built pump room and hotel. Humble cottages were knocked

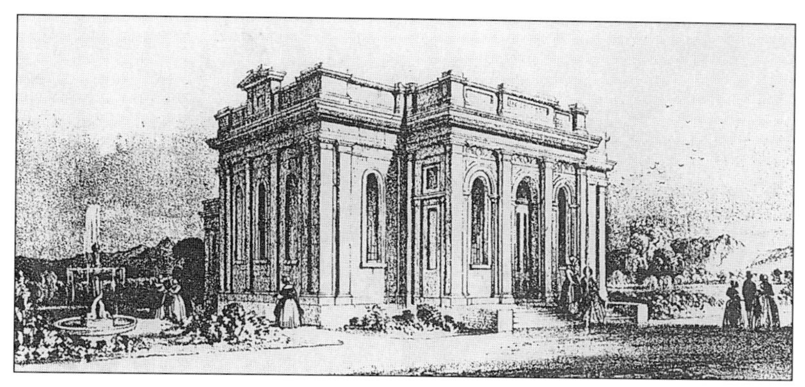

83 The architect's impression of the Pump Room, Hockley Spa. He was obviously unaware of the local environment for there are no large hills to be found in the vicinity of Hockley. It is not known whether the fountain was ever built, 1843.

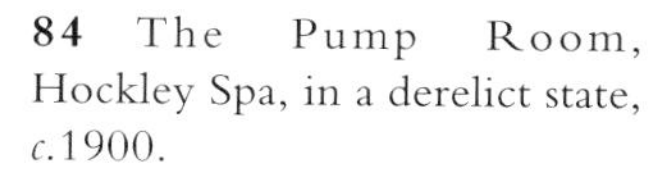

84 The Pump Room, Hockley Spa, in a derelict state, *c.*1900.

down and a number of 'pretty villas' erected. Such was the expectation of a population explosion that it was proposed to erect 10 villa residences and 10 semi-detached villa residences at the rear in order to link the Spa and Southend Roads, and to enlarge the pleasure grounds.

The pump room itself was built in the classical manner and the pump inside was in the form of a Grecian temple. It is a popularly held belief that bathing facilities were available. However, this was never the case; the water was only ever used for drinking. Elegant marble fireplaces stood at each end of the main room, which had painted walls, looking glasses and chandeliers. At the rear of the building was a bottle warehouse and bottling room fitted with apparatus to aerate the water taken directly from the spring. Next to the pump room was a coach house and stables.

The *Spa Hotel* was also built on a grand scale with a sitting room, coffee room, bar,

85 The *Spa Hotel* in about 1910.

86 A clear view down Spa Road and underneath the railway bridge to Greensward Lane. In one of the cottages on the left lived Tommy Horslin, the blacksmith, who walked to Maldon to find work when he could not get any locally.

87 In the early years of the 20th century successful surveyor and land-agent, J.H. Burgess purchased the Pump Room and incorporated it into his new home as a billiard and games room.

88 Spa Road, Hockley. On the right is Mr Burgess' red brick house and on the left, just past the cottages, the entrance to Hockley Station. The railway bridge can just be made out in the distance.

89 Looking down Spa Road to the Pump Room on the right.

parlour, all with marble fireplaces; a kitchen and cold meat larder; and many bedrooms with veneered marble sinks.

But there was one element Mr. Fawcett had not taken into account in his grand design. Not only did people take the waters for their health, but they also wanted entertainment and lots of it. The village of Hockley could not provide the daytime activities available at other spas like Bath and Cheltenham. There were no museums or stately homes to visit and none of the concerts, promenades and grand balls which were part of the social scene elsewhere. Worse still, the public were discovering the pleasures of sea bathing at the new resorts, now so easily accessible since the arrival of the railway. The public did not come.

For years the Spa struggled on, water even being taken by cart to London each day. The story is told of a gentleman from the Maldon area who so firmly believed in the beneficial effects of the Hockley spa water that he sent his servant daily to collect a bottle of it. What he did not know, however, was that the money was spent on drink of the alcoholic kind at the *Hawk Inn*, Battlesbridge, and the bottle was filled with ordinary pump water.

In 1863 the *Spa Hotel*, now known as *The Royal Oak*, was sold to Wells and Perry, later the Chelmsford Brewery, for £350. The inn gained a low reputation and it was from here that the poor of the village received their weekly dole.

In 1873 the pump room was leased as a Baptist chapel for £8 per annum and then in the 1890s it was incorporated as a billiard room into the handsome red brick house built next door. Since that time the building has had a chequered history, being used in the early years of this century as a tea room and for community events and later as shirt and billiard factories. In recent years there were fears that Hockley was about to lose its 'great white elephant', but it has now been bought by a private individual and is in safe hands.

90 *Right.* Looking up Spa Road to Hockley centre.

91 *Below.* The *Spa Hotel* as seen from the Southend Road.

SPA HOTEL

Chapter Nine

Law and Disorder

BEFORE THE FOUNDING of the modern police force, constables were appointed by the parish to keep law and order. Magistrates were drawn from the local gentry but were hard to find, since they preferred to live outside the Rochford Hundred because of its unhealthy climate and unprofitable land. The situation became so bad that in 1770 there were just two elderly justices of the peace for the whole of the Rochford Hundred area who 'sat on the bench' only very occasionally.

At this time there were many more reasons why a person might fall foul of the law. There was the failure of repair roads and ditches, building of cottages without the statutory four acres of land and a whole host of things that could not be done on a Sunday such as playing cards, fiddling and dancing, riding a hobby horse, all of which are mentioned in the court records for Rochford Hundred.

In this day and age it is hard to believe that anyone would go to the trouble of stealing oak trees and not expect to be noticed, but wood was a valuable commodity in the past. In 1567 two unnamed Hockley men were fined 8d. each for digging a trench in the grounds of Edmund Tyrrell's estate at Beeches Manor, Rawreth, and cutting down and taking away two oak trees to the value of 20s. 0d. It is probable that the trees were growing in the hedgerows since Beeches Manor did not have any local woodland.

In October 1575, William Jeffrey of Rawreth was badly assaulted whilst travelling on the highway at Corringham. His attackers were Reynold Peckham and Henry Isley, who used cudgels, swords and fists in an effort to steal from Jeffrey the £24 he was carrying on behalf of Edward Barlett of Hockley.

The poaching of pheasants was such a serious offence that acts for their protection were passed in 1495 and 1541. A fine of £10, an enormous sum in those days, was payable by the defendant, £5 going to the prosecutor and £5 to the owner. Edward Eastwood, a servant of Lord Cobham, who had been staying in an alehouse at Hockley, made the big mistake of getting caught on New Year's Day 1587 in possession of six dead partridge and other fowl. In his defence Eastwood said he had taken the birds at Asheldham (Ashingdon) with the permission of Lord Rich. Needless to say, Lord Rich's bailiff denied having done so.

Someone else's livestock was always a temptation and in 1569 a labourer named Linsell stole six pigs from Thomas Young, a gentleman of Hockley. Fortunately for him their value was only 11d. each. Had they been more, then he would certainly have hanged.

A vicious gang operated in the area led by Edward Hedge the elder and Edward Hedge the younger, both of Hockley. In 1562, together with a gang of eight others, including four from Sutton and Eastwood, they broke into 'Smythes', the home of George Monoux at Sutton, and assaulted him 'putting him in fear of his life'. Unfortunately for George Monoux, his house was broken into again the following year, this time, however, not by the

Hedges. In 1563 the two Hedges were again in trouble having stolen two horses and two foals to the value of £7 and two ewes and three lambs worth 20s. 0d. belonging to Thomas Marten of Prittlewell. They drove the animals to Rochford Park where they were later discovered.

Although no names are given it might just be possible that it was the Hedges' gang, this time including two men from Horseheath, Cambridge, who were responsible for breaking into the garden of John Barnardiston of Hawkwell, assaulting his maidservant and imprisoning her for two hours.

One wonders at the background to the story of Joan, the wife of Bennett Baseley of Hawkwell, who in 1605 was badly beaten by Edward Claydon of Eastwood 'so that she despaired of her life'.

Not attending church on a regular basis was also an offence for which John Couch of Hockley was summoned twice in 1666. It would appear, however, that he was a member of a non-conformist religious group, for the records state that 'under cover of religion they forcibly assembled together'. Ten other defendants stood trial with John, some of whom came from Dagenham and Southchurch.

A one line entry in the court records for 1688 leaves one wondering why William Saffold stole a curtain worth 1s. 0d. from South Fambridge Hall.

The rector of Hawkwell church had a very nasty experience when in 1687 he was 'abused by marines'. Unfortunately the records do not go on to tell us exactly what had happened to the poor man. In 1808 the local police constable was assaulted during a horse race on Hawkwell Common.

With such a lonely and uninhabited landscape it is not surprising that smuggling flourished in the area. The river Crouch, sometimes known as the Burnham River, was ideal for smuggling, being shallow, slow flowing, desolate and with sandbanks along the estuary over which the revenue cutters could not pass. Small vessels would anchor just inside the river and rowing boats put out from the villages along the river bank to meet them. Along the river between Hullbridge and Hockley there is an area known locally as Brandy Hole and tradition has it that this is where the smugglers sank their casks of spirits for later collection. There are the inevitable stories of a passage from the river to *The Bull Inn*, and of secret rooms in the church and behind the fireplace in Costards Woodward, an old house on the Main Road, Hockley. The secret passage to *The Bull* is very unlikely as the landlord was a revenue officer, who on one occasion was beaten up by smugglers and nearly killed. Despite searches no secret rooms have ever been found in Hockley church or at Costards Woodward.

The story is told of a well-to-do landowner who frequently drove to London with £100-worth of lace in his gig. In order to confuse the revenue officers he had his horses' shoes put on the wrong way round so that it looked as if he was travelling in the opposite direction.

In 1840 the Essex Police Force was founded and in 1863 Hockley got its own PC, Frederick Brown. Constable 50 Brown served his community until 1892 when he retired. He was such a popular personality that on his retirement he was presented with an illuminated testimonial scroll signed by all the local residents.

From this time on crime detection becomes more professional. Smart detective work led to the arrest of a burglar who broke into the home of Noah Caplin of Bartons Farm, Lower Road, Hockley, in 1898. Apparently the thief entered by the back sitting room window and stole a gold watch and chain, a £5 bank note, £5 in gold and silver and money belonging to the children, together with meat, puddings, bread, a pair of dark trousers and a vest. A Superintendent Simmons discovered that Caplin, who was a Russian, only employed fellow countrymen on his farm. An old waistcoat was found

92 A photograph of the Rochford Division taken in April 1873. Hockley's PC Frederick Brown is believed to be second from the left in the back row.

93 Constable 50 Frederick Brown in front of the Police House, High Road, Hockley (now Rose Cottage) in approximately 1880. It is just possible to make out the word 'police' picked out in flowers in the front garden. Beneath the house is a cell in which offenders were kept.

which was later identified as having belonged to a man who had worked at the farm some two months before. The superintendent was immediately suspicious and went to the suspect's home address in London to interview him. A search revealed the stolen clothing in his bedroom and the case was solved.

In her book the redoubtable Miss Tawke of Bullwood Hall tells the story of the capture of alleged fowl stealers Herbert Merryfield, Samuel Shelley, Thomas Smith and Henry Wilson in 1890. Apparently Mr. Mark Wendon heard suspicious noises in his stable so he locked the door and sent for the police. Until they came he and his daughter, Elizabeth, kept guard together with two servants with double-barrelled shotguns. Elizabeth herself had a revolver! When the police arrived they found Smith, Wilson and Shelley under some hay and Merryfield hiding in a chaff bin. Two large bags were found from which those present concluded that the four trespassers had been on their way to the nearby fowl house to steal the chickens. When questioned Merryfield said they had been going to Hockley but it had come on to rain and they had sheltered in the stable. Several other charges for trespass and theft having been taken into account, when the case came to court Merryfield got 21 days hard labour, Shelley and Smith 14 and Wilson seven. Miss Tawke reports that 'The prisoners left the dock smiling.'

Alfred Griggs, Lewis Tate and George Whitwell paid a high price for the mushrooms

94 This photograph clearly demonstrates how much a part of life rabbit hunting was to rural communities. On this occasion the hunter is doing so quite legally. The photograph was taken in what is now the centre of Hockley village.

they stole in 1898 from wealthy landowner and justice of the peace, Samuel Baker. Although the mushrooms were valued at only 12s. 0d., Griggs was fined 10s. 0d. with 8s. 4d. costs and 4s. 0d. damages and both Tate and Whitwell were sentenced to 14 days' hard labour.

In a country area, trespass and poaching were a way of life. Little mercy was shown if the poacher was found at the scene of the crime, as happened to brickmaker Benjamin Hart. In 1901 Benjamin was caught red-handed by landowner, Mr. T.W. Offin, and his groom whilst shooting rabbits in Hockley Woods. Not only was Hart apprehended but his dog was killed, being shot no less than three times. To make matters worse, Hart then tried to drive off one of the men's horses, claiming it in compensation for his dog. Hart's plea that he had only climbed over the fence to retrieve his dog was not believed and he was fined 10s. 0d. with 10s. 0d. costs.

Ernest Leek, an engineer, and his brother-in-law George Gibson, a labourer, were also apprehended whilst 'going in search of rabbits' in Woodham Ferrers. They had crossed the river at Hullbridge, carrying their bicycles, and then cycled on to the farm of Ernest Cockleston. Here they were seen hiding behind a fence and later walking along the road under the railway bridge. When challenged they refused to give their names, and the constable was called. They then picked up their bicycles and rode off as quickly as they could towards Hullbridge. In defence Leek said that he had been taking the dogs over to see friends at South Woodham Ferrers and Althorne and had only been resting on the farmer's land. Needless to say the magistrates were sceptical and Leek was fined £1 and Gibson £1 2s. 6d.

In October 1936, Dennis Crawford Woolley of the Balsham Poultry Farm, Hullbridge, was charged with obtaining 13s. 6d. by false pretences from Frank Strain, an auctioneer at Rayleigh. Apparently the defendant had arranged for Strain to auction a quantity of eggs at Rayleigh Market and signed a card stating that they were English and new laid. However, the sanitary inspector who checked them found 14 dozen of the eggs were unfit for human consumption. Later the police visited Woolley's farm where they found more foreign bad eggs, together with preserving chemicals.

Chapter Ten

Inns

FOR SUCH A LARGE AREA there are remarkably few public houses or inns. Those that do exist are to be found on the main transport links. We have already mentioned the *Spa Hotel* and *The Bull* at Hockley, the *White Hart* on the village green at Hawkwell, all on the turnpike road, and *The Anchor* at Hullbridge near to the river crossing.

However, until approximately the late 1860s there was one more—*The Drovers* on the Hockley/Rayleigh border. As its name implies, *The Drovers* was a stopping place for sheep drovers and cattle men *en route* to the cattle markets at Rochford, Wickford, Chelmsford and Stanford-le-Hope. A substantial building with a number of outhouses and pens for the livestock,

95 The *Bull Inn*, Hockley, *c.*1910. Note the chickens in the middle of what is now the B1013, one of the busiest roads in south-east Essex!

96 Another view of the *Bull Inn*, taken a few years later. By now Hockley has become a popular place to visit for a day out and the inn and the cottage opposite are both selling teas for the visitors.

97 Looking up the Hawkwell Road to the *White Hart*, which is the last building on the right facing on to the common. Note the muddy and rutted road, today the frantically busy B1013. Approximately 1910.

98 The *Anchor Inn*, Hullbridge, showing the river crossing. This Essex weather-boarded building was demolished to make way for the present *Anchor* which faces the river. Note the bus parked to the side of the building.

99 The wedding photograph of George and Ellen Prior taken at the *Drovers Inn* in 1886. The wedding took place at Rayleigh church, but only after a relative had rushed back to Leigh on Sea to retrieve the wedding ring which the bridegroom had forgotten.

100 The *Drovers Inn* was considerably altered prior to becoming a private residence. It was demolished in the 1960s.

it was open practically all day selling beer, but no wines or spirits, and providing simple food such as bread and cheese. There was one speciality of the house, jam puffs, of which there was always a generous supply.

Accommodation for the travellers was basic, often no more than a pile of hay in the stables. The kitchen was outside and all the cooking was done by a maid on the open fire. The drinking arrangements were segregated. The locals drank in the bar parlour, whilst the drovers made do with the sand-covered floor of the taproom. It was the custom at that time for a person who had been on the road for two miles to qualify as 'a traveller', and receive a drink before the locals.

The landlord in 1887 was Samuel Bowen, a member of a large family who held the tenancies of several public houses in the area. His son went on to become the licensee of *The Bull* at Hockley. Eventually *The Drovers* became a private house, until the early 1960s, when it was bought by a builder and demolished to make way for the Gattens development. Although the inn may have gone, its name is not forgotten for that particular stretch of the Rayleigh Road is still known as 'Drovers Hill'.

Drink was the scourge of agricultural communities such as Hockley and Hawkwell at the end of the last century. Hours were long, work was hard and often lonely, and men found companionship and comfort in the local inns. Labourers expected to receive daily beer from their farmers, especially at threshing time when gallon bottles or 4½-gallon casks were supplied for the refreshment of the workers. A bottle of Irish whisky cost 3s. 6d., a crate of brown ale 2s. 6d., a quart of cider 4d., ginger beer 1d. and lemonade ¾d. Licensing hours were long, 6 a.m-10 p.m., and unemployed men often found it more convivial to sit in front of the pub's roaring fire all day drinking beer at ¾d. and eating bread and cheese for 2d., whilst at home their families were starving. If the customer had no money then a tally was kept on a slate over the bar.

At the *White Hart Inn*, Hawkwell, it was possible for customers to buy half a bullock's head for 1s. 6d. or a sheep's head for 6d. The heads were then put in a huge communal iron boiler over a fire in the taproom (if you wanted to be served you had to 'tap' for attention) with vegetables, and simmered for 2-3 hours. Unfortunately there were always those who could not wait until the meat was cooked and would help themselves out of the pot, later complaining to the landlord, 'That's funny, the meat has boiled off the bones'!

The pub was also the place for financial transactions and wages for agricultural workers were paid at the *White Hart*.

Chapter Eleven

The Great Land Sales

THE ARRIVAL of the Great Eastern railway brought dramatic changes to the area. Hockley, Hawkwell and Hullbridge changed from small scattered agricultural communities into the overgrown villages we know today. If Hockley could be said to have had a 'centre' at all at that time it was around the parish church, but as the lie of the land in that area was not suitable for the building of a station, it was constructed some two miles away to the east.

Wadham College, Oxford was one of the first landowners to benefit financially, when in 1887 it sold land at Hockley Hall to the value of £276 to the Great Eastern Railway for the construction of the track.

Many of the local landowners grasped the opportunity to sell their estates for development, and farms that had existed since medieval times were broken up and sold plot by plot. One of the first to go was Hyams Farm, Hawkwell, in April 1894. As the land gradually disappeared under housing a field was retained for use by the Hawkwell Football Club. In turn this piece of land, in what was to be called Hyams Road, became the bowls club.

In August 1894 Mr. Offin of Turrett House, Hockley, offered 62 plots of land on what was to become the Bullwood estate, Hockley. The auction took place in the *Spa Hotel* and 'following lively competition', as a newspaper article of the time put it, plots 31 ft. by 125ft., with frontage sold for £40. Purchasers came from far and wide and a Mr. Savage of East Ham alone bought 22 of the woodland plots with garden sites for £240. Sid Horslin and his wife Flo took the opportunity to buy a plot for £40 which they later turned into the popular Hockley Tea Gardens.

Prospective purchasers were usually treated to luncheon and drink flowed freely, as was the case in October 1894, when 290 plots were offered for sale on the Hockley Hill estate. Incentives to purchase were offered and in July 1901, when the London Road estate, Hockley, came on to the market, local builder Bysouth advertised payment by instalments, free conveyancing, 5 per cent discount for cash and free railway rides!

It was the sale of Kiln Farm by the Fellows and Scholars of Christ's College, Cambridge, that was to centralise Hockley. Kiln Farm, as the name implies, had grown up on the old brick fields opposite the *Spa Hotel*, fronting the Rochford Road, and included many acres of woodland stretching as far as Hawkwell. The farm did not flourish and in August 1905 the first sale of plots on the Spa estate, as it was called, took place in a marquee, with lunch provided. Conveniently close to the railway station, the plots went for £25 each with a special price of 10 for £200. Other sales took place in 1907 and 1921.

In 1906 the ancient farm of Smythe and Snares, formerly Chamberlains, located to the west of Greensward Lane, Ashingdon, came on to the market. Such was the size of the estate that for sales purposes it was divided into two halves—the south being land in

101 The Hawkwell Football Team, 1906-7.

102 Harrogate House, formerly the ancient Smythe and Snares Farm, *c.*1960.

HOCKLEY, Essex.

A Short Distance from the Important Town of Southend-on-Sea.

Close to Rochford, and only 1½ miles from the well-known Boating and Yachting River Crouch. The District is rapidly developing and becoming a favourite residential part for London business men and others.

THE HARROGATE PARK ESTATE

practically adjoining the HOCKLEY RAILWAY STATION, whence there are frequent trains to Southend, and a good, fast and cheap service to London, via., Brentwood Ilford and Stratford.

MESSRS.

PAYNE, TRAPPS & Co.

Will Sell by Auction, in a Marquee upon the Estate,

On MONDAY, APRIL 29th, 1907,

At TWO o'clock,

71 Valuable Freehold Sites,

Ripe for the erection of BUNGALOW and VILLA RESIDENCES.

The Roads will, be well formed. Free of Cost.

Sold Free of Tithe. No Law Costs. Ten per cent. deposit. Balance by Instalments if desired. Five per cent. discount for Cash.

THE RAILWAY SERVICE IS GOOD. SEASON TICKETS ABOUT 10d. PER DAY.

Affording a Grand Opportunity for Investment. The Water Main is laid past Estate.

Intending Purchasers will leave Liverpool Street Main Line on day of Sale by the 12 o'clock train, calling at Stratford 12.10. Also from Southend-on-Sea (G.E.R.) at 1.35.

LUNCHEON WILL BE PROVIDED.

Full particulars may be obtained of :—The SPA HOTEL, HOCKLEY ; Messrs. MILLS, CURRY & GASKELL, Solicitors, 11, Queen Victoria Street, E.C., and Messrs. PAYNE, TRAPPS & Co., Auctioneers, 11, Queen Victoria Street, E.C. Telephone, 6008 Bank.

103 Sale particulars on behalf of Payne, Trapps & Co. for the sale of Harrogate Park Estate, April 1907.

The Harrogate Park Building Estate.

HOCKLEY, Essex.

REMARKS.

HOCKLEY has a growing repute for its healthy and invigorating air reminding one, on its Northern slopes of the bracing effects of a visit to Scotland without its attendant expense. There is a Public Hall, Post and Telegraph Office, and the Spa Hotel (originally erected for the use of visitors drinking the Spa Water).

THE HARROGATE PARK ESTATE practically adjoins the Railway Station.

ON THE DIRECT SOUTHEND LINE of the G.E.R., only about six miles from that favorite Seaside Resort with the advantage of a good service of trains, whence the City is easily reached at extremely moderate fares.

CONSIDERABLE DEVELOPMENT is taking place at Hockley, many new Houses have lately been erected, and building is still proceeding, which points to a prosperous and improving future for land in this locality.

THE WATER MAINS are laid past the Estate.

104 Advertising the merits of the Harrogate Park Building Estate.

Hockley and the north in Ashingdon. The Hockley lands were the first to go under the hammer and on 29 April 1906 Messrs. Payne, Trapps and Co. held the first auction of 71 freehold sites in what was called the Harrogate Park estate. The sale was a success, attended by a large number of people. After a fine lunch and despite a heavy thunderstorm which limited a trip to view the estate, five main-road plots were sold for a total of £185. Five further plots in the future Hamilton Gardens were disposed of for £19 each. The second sale took place on 3 May, again in Hamilton Gardens, after which an article in a local newspaper noted how pleasant it was to see that so many local people were purchasers. Yet another auction took place on 17 May, when the same newspaper pointed out that there were only 30 plots left and therefore the price was rising! The final sale was held on 24 May, when the 35 plots on offer realised £460 10s. 0d. The disposal of this huge area of land meant that the majority of Hockley's population, which had until then been confined to the south of the railway line, now extended across the countryside to the north. Following their success in Hockley, Payne, Trapps and Co. went on to sell the north portion of the farm in Ashingdon and from there to the Hockley View estate!

After a gap of four years Messrs. Payne, Trapps and Co. were back in Hockley, this time to sell land to the west of Hockley Hall on behalf of Wadham College. A plan exists which shows that it was intended to auction 274 plots, but the venture fell through, fortunately for modern Hockley residents, as such a development would have destroyed what is now one of the most attractive views in the area.

The suitability of land for future development was often used as an incentive to tempt prospective purchasers of large estates when they came on to the market. In 1902 Marsh Farm, South Fambridge was up for sale. Although on the north bank of the Crouch, the farm still came within the parish of Hockley. In the sales catalogue it was described as 'ripe for building upon' and emphasis was placed on its nearness to South Woodham Ferrers railway station.

105 View from Hockley church of the land which Wadham College had hoped to sell in 274 lots for development in 1910. Fortunately the venture fell through.

In 1913 Mr. Offin of Turrett House died and his vast landholdings came on to the market. Not only had he owned Turrett House, Hockley, but also Raymonds and Dollymans farms, Rawreth; Cranes Farm, Nevedon; Fryerns Farm, Nevedon and Basildon; Wick Farm, Vange; The Pitsea Ten Acres, Pitsea and building land at Rayleigh. As can be imagined, the sales catalogue is extensive and makes fascinating reading. It is pointed out that the Turrett House land is ripe for conversion into building estates and is within easy distance of the Great Eastern and Midlands Railway and that season tickets cost £3 15s. 3d. per quarter, or 10d. per day. Fortunately, Turrett House was never sold on for future development.

Costards Woodward, on the Main Road, Hockley, was offered for sale in 1923. The auctioneer's catalogue includes information on a large number of outbuildings and land which 'could be used for development'. It also notes that 'with the rapid development of Hockley and the surrounding district the property is sure to grow in value'. The auctioneer was correct; as time went on the land was developed but fortunately this lovely old house still remains.

Even before the increased development in the area, the demand for bricks had been growing and as a result a number of brick kilns had been built locally. Hockley's first brick kiln, in Tudor times, is believed to have been in the vicinity of Folly Lane and it is from here that the bricks to build the church porch are thought to have come. The disused kiln at Kiln Farm, Hockley, has already been mentioned, and in response to increased demand a new kiln commenced operation to the south of the railway line in the early years of the 20th century making the red, but rather soft, brick that is to be seen in buildings throughout the area. This kiln is now the site of the Elden Way Trading Estate. At Hullbridge a kiln was built alongside the river and there were two others on the Hawkwell/ Rochford borders.

Not all of the land that came up for sale was built on immediately as many of the purchasers lived in London and elsewhere and viewed their newly acquired piece of the countryside only as weekend and holiday retreats. A hotch potch of dwellings arose at the end of unmade roads ranging from little more than sheds and converted railway carriages to sophisticated wooden bungalows. As with so much of south-east Essex, Hockley, Hawkwell and Hullbridge had entered the 'plotland' era.

106 This photograph of Grasmere Avenue, Hullbridge, clearly illustrates the variety of dwellings that arose as a result of plotland development, *c*.1920.

107 Coventry Corner, Hullbridge. As there was little centralised building control, dwellings of all varieties arose, sometimes in the most inappropriate places. Coventry Corner, with its shop, was built in the middle of open countryside, *c*.1930.

108 Plumberow Avenue, Hockley. Originally the access to Plumberow Farm, when the land was sold for development a number of attractive bungalows were built along what was no more than a cart track. Probably 1930s.

109 *Left.* A view of the bungalows built along Folly Lane, Hockley, when the lands of Folly Farm (the tall building at the end) were sold, *c.*1930.

110 *Below.* A hardly recognisable view of the High Road, Hockley, *c.*1920.

111 Standing in lonely isolation, Doris Villa, Greensward Lane, Hockley, which was later to become the home of Hockley's first doctor, Dr. Morgan, and remained a surgery until the 1980s.

112 This photograph shows some fine examples of the extravagant architecture to be seen in the Hockley area in the early 1900s. Despite the sophisticated buildings, the road is only a grass track. Station Road area.

Chapter Twelve

Development and Change

AS MORE AND MORE of the plots were built on and became permanent homes, many residents found themselves marooned along muddy tracks. Even as late as 1965 there were still 33 miles of unmade roads in the Rochford area. It was at this time that new developments on the site of the recently demolished Plumberow Manor, Hockley, and nearby roads resulted in Plumberow Avenue becoming a sea of mud. Local residents were undergoing real hardship as doctors and mid-wives had difficulty getting to their patients and it was impossible for any large vehicles—including fire engines, ambulances, hearses—to get down the muddy track. Children had to negotiate dangerous, unhealthy conditions on the way to school and there was the constant fear that a builder's lorry might overturn and cause serious injury or death. Rochford Rural District Council was unsympathetic as they claimed that the road was historically a foot-path and therefore not their responsibility. In response the residents took the matter into their own hands and the women formed a pressure group which soon gained national media coverage. Petitions were signed and a letter

113 The development of the shops at Apex corner and the building of a council estate and police houses in the 1964, turned Plumberow Avenue, Hockley, into a sea of mud. The road to the left is Plumberow Mount Avenue.

10 Downing Street
Whitehall

March 12, 1965.

Dear Mrs. [illegible]urt,

The Prime Minister has asked me to reply to your letter about the making up of Plumberow Avenue, Hockley, and connected roads.

Mr. Wilson is advised that no Minister of the Crown has any power either to require a street works authority to make up a street, or to intervene in the way an authority carries out the procedure of the private street works codes; Parliament has left these functions to the authority's discretion.

He understands that the Rochford Rural District Council, with the help of the Essex County Council, are making good progress in the research necessary to prepare a reply to the contention of objectors to the scheme that Plumberow Avenue is not a private street, and that the objections will be referred to the magistrates for determination as soon as possible.

He understands also that the rural district council take the view that to carry out street works now in any of the four streets leading off Plumberow Avenue for which schemes have been prepared would result in making the condition of Plumberow Avenue worse. They therefore do not consider it wise to make up those side roads in advance of Plumberow Avenue itself.

Yours sincerely,

The Honorary Secretary,
Plumberow Area Residents (Ladies) Association.

114 Letter received from Prime Minister Wilson's office following the residents' letter drawing his attention to the appalling state of Plumberow Avenue.

115 The ladies of the Plumberow Avenue area working to clear a way through the mud, 1965.

116 Main Road, Hockley, *c.*1910. The shops on the left-hand side of the picture were a barber's and Gurney's haberdashers. Just visible to the right is the entrance to Horslin's shop.

taken to the Prime Minister, Harold Wilson, at Downing Street. In desperation the women placed planks with six-inch nails in them on the road to stop the construction traffic and, in an effort to shame the council, 60 housewives, the eldest 80 and five of them pregnant, set to with shovels, buckets and wheel-barrows in a bid to remove some of the surface mud from the road. In May 1965 the matter was taken to court and the judge ruled that historically Plumberow Avenue, as far as Plumberow Mount, was a highway and the authorities were therefore responsible for its upkeep. However, the part of Plumberow past the Mount was no more than a footpath, and so it has remained to this day.

Boundary disputes were common and often ended in court. In March 1923 Arthur and Alwyn Fynch of The Plot, Hullbridge and Alfred Victor of Pevensey Gardens, Hockley were summoned for removing a fence, post and gate to the value of £3 with a pickaxe. The landowner, a Mr. Smith, armed himself with a truncheon and a fight ensued. The two Fynches also admitted they had deposited soot on the waterfront, but in support of their case stated that 'no bathers had complained of damaged clothing'.

Shops were built to supply an urban population used to purchasing the necessities of life. Despite this new competition, W. Heddle of 32 Park Street, Southend, an itinerant tradesman, continued to visit the Hockley area until the First World War and his account books give an interesting insight into the needs of the ladies of the village. For instance in 1914, Mrs Nice of Main Road purchased a blouse for 5s. 6d., 9 yards of material for 5s. 0d., one dozen buttons for 2d. and a corset for 1s. 11d. Miss Wood, described as living near the station, Main Road, bought one bloomer for 1s. 11d, gloves for 1s. 0d. and

117 Main Road, Hockley looking towards the *Spa Hotel*, *c*.1900.

118 Inifer Potter's shop, 1913. Note the variety of merchandise and the boy with the delivery bicycle.

119 Looking down Spa Road, *c.*1920. The landau outside the *Spa Hotel* belonged to Mr. Lark who would in the near future open a garage in Spa Road. Note the lack of shops on the right-hand side of Spa Road.

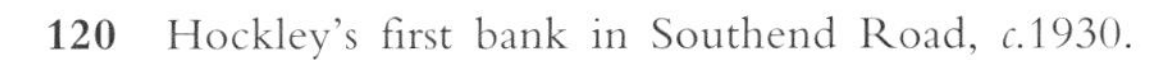
120 Hockley's first bank in Southend Road, *c.*1930.

121 Nicholson's the shoe menders, Southend Road, Hockley. Note his leather apron. Nobles bakery was at the rear, *c.*1913.

122 The water tower, Pooles Lane, Hullbridge.

her new corset, obviously a more fashionable model than Mrs. Nice's, cost 2s. 11d. Skirts, boots, dresses, blankets, eiderdowns, quilts, bolsters and towels were also offered for sale.

Many smallholdings and nurseries grew up in the area. Fresh fruit and vegetables were grown for sale in Southend, and flowers were sent by train to London for the big houses of the city. Seeing an ideal opportunity to advertise his wares, one nurseryman took over the railway station gardens and until very recently one single rose from that time managed to survive beside the down platform. During the popular Southend Illuminations, local women, dressed as gypsies, did a brisk trade selling bunches of flowers to the visitors.

So much *ad hoc* development, without any thought for the requirements of an infrastructure, caused many problems in those early days, particularly with the supply of fresh water. In 1895 Hockley Parish Council gave permission to erect a pump over the spring at Greensward Lane, and the well was deepened and domed over. The well on land next to Hockley church was to receive similar treatment. Two years later, in 1897, the council agreed that a pump, to be known as the Jubilee pump, should be erected on waste land by the roadside on the common. Although the water mains came through Hockley in the early years of the century, for the majority of people water came from the well or was delivered by cart. One elderly Hockley resident, now in her 90s, can remember as a child having to collect water in buckets from the well at the farm where Broad Parade now stands. Her cottage opposite the Old Pump Room did not even have a well.

Hullbridge had a particularly serious problem. Due to the poor quality, water had to be carted to the village. Hockley's water main terminated at Hockley church and it was from a standpipe here that the water cart filled up for its journey to Hullbridge. For many years the residents of Hullbridge campaigned through public meetings and petitions for their

123 'Thistledown', Folly Chase, Hockley, one of the many nurseries that opened due to the availability of cheap land and easily accessible markets in Southend and via the railway to London

124 Wedding photograph of Victor and Elizabeth Baldry taken on 13 June 1914. Victor spent two years of his army service in Rawal Pindi in India. He was demobbed in 1920. In 1927 he bought some land in Hawkwell, built a bungalow and started a nursery which he named Rawal Pindi.

125 Mill Hill, Church Road, Hockley, the home of well known Southend and London florist, Mr. Longman. Once a year he invited all his staff and their families to his house for a day in the country, *c.*1925.

own water supply. Even into the late 1920s Hullbridge was still waiting for a supply of fresh water.

With no sewerage system there were continuous problems of cesspits overflowing into ditches and across gardens, and frequent complaints were made to the parish council about the terrible smells in the centre of Hockley. One Hawkwell resident (now sadly deceased) used to tell how he and his brother emptied the cesspits, a job that had to be done twice a year. As it was illegal to empty a cesspit during daylight hours, they would start the work after a long day in the fields, rarely finishing before 3 or 4 a.m. A large pit could take as long as 3-4 hours to empty, much of the time using only a bucket on the end of a rope. For this heavy and unpleasant work they were only paid between £1 10s. and £2. After they had finished the job they would go home and scrub-up as best they could—there was no bath in the house. He also told the story of how he set a cesspit (and nearly himself) on fire. Apparently, in the dark he removed a can from the cover of the pit they were about to empty. He could not see what it contained, but it was either paraffin or petrol. What he did not know was that the can had been leaking into the cesspit. When he lit a match to look down into the pit it exploded. Not only did the brothers empty pits, but they also dug them. They had to be at least 8-10 ft. deep and at the end all they received was £1 5s.

126 Mr. Prior, Hockley's lamplighter, in his garden at China Cottage, Spa Road in 1913.

In 1912 the parish council contracted for a sewerage cart to collect the 'night soil', but obviously this measure could go only a little way towards solving the problem. Hullbridge's situation became desperate when in 1911 pails were substituted for the 'old closets' and the parish clerk wrote to the Rochford Rural Council seeking assistance. We do not know what happened in this particular situation, but in 1936 Hullbridge was still having problems and formed its own residents' association, which proposed that the village should join with Rayleigh whose sewerage system passed nearby 'as very few people went to Hockley for anything'.

Hockley got its first street lights in January 1899, which stretched from the railway bridge, next to the railway station, to the post office. A lamplighter, Mr. Prior, was employed at £6 a year to light the oil lamps between October and February. He also had to maintain the lamps and take them down and store them during the summer months. At the same time as Hockley installed its lamps, so did Hullbridge—just one! The oil lamps remained until 1923 when the gas main was laid. Hockley boasted six new lights at a total cost of £56: one at the entrance to Folly Lane, one in Hall Road, one opposite the path across the Cromwell estate, two in Station Road and the last at the entrance to Fountain Lane. By 1923 the village had 32 new electric lights with power laid on by the

127 Hockley Public Hall.

County of London Electricity Supply Co. Inevitably some residents complained that they were not happy with electricity and wanted to remain with gas! According to them the lighting in Hockley was 'deplorable'.

A growing population needed somewhere to meet and play, and in 1902 Mrs. Augusta Mary Tawke of Whitbreads gave the community two plots of land in Bullwood Road, Hockley, on which was to be built a hall to be used for meetings, as a reading room and library. The Public Hall, as it was known, soon became the centre of the community and was used for a variety of events. One of the first organisations to hold regular meetings there was the Women's Institute and in 1925 they celebrated their Christmas party with masked carollers, attired in scarlet cloaks and hoods, whilst other members recited and put on a sketch. In 1926 the entertainment included a mannequin parade, a cookery talk and at the end of the meeting the members collected £1 16s. 0d. for distressed minors. Not all the events held at the Public Hall were purely social and it frequently provided a venue for church services. In November 1936 a united service was held there with the British Legion, Scouts and Guides, marching from the *Spa Hotel* to the hall. In his address the Rev. Budd said, 'that the peace making efforts of the last 15 years had come to nought and that the League of Nations was discredited.' Following the address the roll of honour for the fallen for Hockley and Hawkwell was read. The hall was damaged by a landmine during the Second World War, but it was repaired and the opportunity taken to extend it. The Public Hall still plays an important part in the life of the community of Hockley, but it is growing old and plans are in hand for its modernisation following an encouraging lottery grant.

The first reference in the area to a post office is at Hockley in 1902, when it was noted that the letters were frequently late and doubt was cast on the ability of the post master to take on the proposed telegraph work. Originally the post office was open from 8 a.m. to 8 p.m., but by 1912 it had started closing on Wednesday afternoons, although stamps could be bought at the door. Perhaps there were complaints about the service, for in 1931, although the half-day working on a Wednesday continued, letters could be delivered and collected by callers between 5-5.30 p.m.

128 Hockley Post Office and staff, Southend Road, 1913.

In 1935 a group of local residents became concerned that Hockley, now growing into a sizeable village, would be vulnerable if a serious fire should occur. As the nearest services were at Rochford and Rayleigh, they decided to take matters into their own hands and formed their own volunteer fire brigade. A second-hand Morris lorry was acquired, painted bright red and modified to carry the men and equipment. The proprietor of the *Spa Hotel* offered garaging in what had originally been the hotel stables. It took a while to acquire the necessary equipment and at first they only had stirrup pumps and stand-pipe keys to open fire hydrants. Sixteen volunteers, most of them local, came forward and six jackets, six leather helmets and six pairs of boots were purchased second-hand from the Liverpool Fire Salvage Company. The first six men to arrive at the Spa Yard were therefore the ones to get the uniforms and go to the fire. Needless to say there was fierce competition to get there first! Just before the outbreak of the Second World War a new fire station was built in Southend Road and in September 1939 the fire brigade became the Auxiliary Fire Service. The Hockley brigade served with particular distinction when the Shell Haven Refinery caught fire. Hockley's captain, Bob Alexander, instructed his men to direct their hoses on the nearby tanks, stopping them from overheating and exploding. As Hockley and Hawkwell grew it became obvious that the Hockley fire station was inadequate and a new one was built at a cost of £42,186 in Hawkwell, where it still is today. It is a matter of pride to the community that the service is still manned by 'retained', volunteer, fire fighters.

Hullbridge gained in popularity as a mini-seaside resort and people came to walk in the country, sail and swim in the river. Unfortunately many did not appreciate how treacherous the river Crouch can be and

129 Hockley's first fire engine, a second-hand Morris lorry, 1935. The Captain, Bob Alexander, is on the far right, behind the bell, and has a white flash on his helmet to denote his rank.

130 Hockley's purpose-built fire station, Southend Road, Hockley. Built on land purchased from the Poores Charity. Note the hoses hanging from the hose tower in the background, 1939. Building now converted for use by the parish council.

131 *Above.* Hockley Auxiliary Fire Service in 1940. Those in uniform are wearing leather boots known as 'Cotton Oxfords' and their jackets are made of Milton cloth. The men to the right are in overalls as they have been on cleaning duty.

132 *Above right.* Swimming in the dangerous waters of the river Crouch, Hullbridge, 1920s.

133 *Right.* The tranquil countryside which visitors came to enjoy at Hullbridge, *c.*1920. Pooles Lane.

134 The caravan park, Hockley. Built on the site of the old brick works, Spa Road, the caravan park existed until the 1970s when it was removed and an old people's home was built. Caravan parks can still be found at Hullbridge, The Dome, Hockley and a planning application was refused for one at Plumberow Avenue as late as 1966.

135 The 'unspoilt Essex village by the River Crouch at Hullbridge' referred to by a correspondent to a local paper in 1934. Ferry Road about 1920. The mission hall is on the left of the picture.

136 Broad Parade, Hockley, 1950s. A parade of shops built to supply the needs of the Broadlands housing estate and other new developments in the area of Greensward Lane.

drownings were not uncommon. On Whitsun Bank Holiday 1936, Charles Alfred Ashley, 18, a metal worker from Peckham, visited Hullbridge with a party of friends. He had only just walked into the river for a swim when he was caught by the tide and swept away. Despite their efforts his friends and the ferryman, Arthur Hymas, could not reach him. At the coroner's inquest Mr Hymas reported that in his 15 years as a ferryman he had rescued as many as thirty people who would otherwise have drowned. On the previous bank holiday he had helped rescue no less than seven swimmers.

Change did not suit everyone as a letter, written to a local paper in 1934, demonstrates:

> I live in what ten years ago was an unspoiled Essex village by the River Crouch at Hullbridge; four years ago it was still a beauty spot, but in this year of a highly developed civilisation it is fast becoming hideous, especially in its most charming spot by the river wall, bank and foreshore. The land has been sold and erections are now appearing as haphazard as they will be ugly, in place of the uncultivated scrub and trees which provided a wild preserve of peace and seclusion, as well as protection of a kind to the bank. No longer will happy children be able to mudlark at low tide on the foreshore, play hide-and-seek on the bank and dress after bathing there unless a miracle happens or the town planning authorities and the Essex Rivers Catchment Board do their duty. The irony is that the part affected comes under two town planning schemes—urban and rural district councils and there is, I believe a Lord of the Manor. And there is a Council for the Preservation of Rural England, but in these parts soon there will be nothing left for its members to have an interest in or to preserve—except water. I write because the same thing may happen in other parts of Essex.

What the above correspondent did not appreciate is that change is inevitable. History is all about change. Although he would find difficulty in recognising the Hullbridge of today, the writer would no doubt be relieved to see that not all the open countryside around his village has vanished under development, as he feared. A walk along the river is still a delight, although no one would swim in it nowadays! Hockley has grown into a small commuter town, despite which it has some of the best countryside and views in the area. Although Hawkwell has increased in size, it still has its two very separate communities, with plenty of green countryside in between.

Chapter Thirteen

War

THE VILLAGE OF ASHINGDON (Assandun) abuts both Hockley and Hawkwell and tradition has it that it was here in 1016 that the invading Danish king, Canute, took on the might of the English army of King Edmund Ironside, and won. Just how involved local people were in the fighting is not known, but no doubt many Hockley and Hawkwell men would have taken part and the local population suffered the misfortunes of a conquered people. It is said that after the battle King Canute built a 'white church' in thanksgiving for his victory and that church was SS Peter and Paul, Hockley. Experts, however, are of the opinion that this was more likely to have been St Andrew's Minster at Ashingdon which overlooks the supposed site of the battle.

There is no documentary evidence to suggest that the villagers of the Rochford Hundred suffered particular hardship as a result of the Norman Conquest, as Swein, the English lord who administered most of the country around and about from his castle at Rayleigh, was a supporter of William of Normandy. They could not have failed to notice a change in their lives, though, as the English tenants of the manors were replaced with Norman French-speaking occupants and the feudal system was strengthened.

Fortunately for Hockley and Hawkwell the various civil wars and strifes of future centuries also passed by, as the area lacked any towns of commercial or financial significance, major population centres, strategic routes or military installations. Benton in his *History of the Rochford Hundred* relates a story current in the 1880s that the bridge at Hullbridge was finally demolished in the Civil War between Charles I and Parliament. He says that it was blown up by the Parliamentarians and cites as evidence the retrieval of a musket from the river bed. Apparently when the musket was cleaned the powder was dry and it could still be fired! As this was a major river crossing there would no doubt have been much coming and going of rival bands during this period. However, there is no historical record of the bridge having been blown up (if indeed it still existed at that time) or of any engagements in the area which, like the majority of Essex, supported the Parliamentary cause.

Things stayed relatively peaceful until the coming of the 20th century and modern warfare. On 2 September 1914, the chairman of the parish councils read out a letter from the Mayor of Southend with a call to arms, and Hockley and Hawkwell went to war.

Concern over the food supply led to the setting up of the Essex Agricultural War Committee, and under the supervision of the parish councils allotments sprang up throughout the area. The owners of the land received £5 a year, whilst the tenants were charged 8d. a rod, a now outdated land measurement of 5½ yards. Vandalism was a common problem with children trespassing and doing damage. In an effort to keep them out of the allotments on Spa Meadow in the centre of Hockley, barbed wire was erected and the police were called.

137 First World War soldiers.

THE RESIDENTS OF HOCKLEY
AND OF HAWKWELL TOO
SEND GREETINGS SINCERE
FOR THE COMING NEW YEAR,
TO OUR LADS IN KHAKI & BLUE.

TO Pte H. Cocks

WITH BEST WISHES FROM OLD ACQUAINTANCES

138 Postcards like this were sent out in their thousands during the First World War to encourage local men serving in the forces.

139 Hockley, Hawkwell and Eastwood as Hitler would have seen them. Luftwaffe photograph taken in the Second World War. Hockley Woods is to the centre with the village and Spa Road, passing under the railway, easily discernible, at the top. Hawkwell is to the right and the plotland at the bottom of the picture is Eastwood. (Reproduced by permission of Rochford District Council.)

140 Hawkwell's 'B' platoon, Home Guard, photographed in Major Hedges' garden, Tudor Way, Hawkwell. The platoon met at Cottons Farm once, opposite Hawkwell Common and the *White Hart*. From left to right starting in the back row: Barlow, Evans, Munns; second back: —, Haken, Abrahams, —, —, —; middle row: —, —, —, —, Sanderson, —, Jim Tanner; second front: —, Robinson, Oates, Major Hedges, J. Williams, —, Harding, Hooker, —; front: —, —, Williams, John Gray.

141 Hockley 'A' platoon, Home Guard met in the old school house next to the church which was strategically placed to overlook the Crouch valley. Included in the photograph taken on Aldermans Hill, Hockley, are Browning?, Bates, Harry Cocks, Jack Riding, Frank Baldwin, Eric Mills?, Shorto?, Major Bion?, Mrs. Harvey?, Alderman Harvey? and Clarence Bourne.

Although not all the men were called up immediately, it was difficult to resist the aggressive recruiting drives taking place locally. Regiments of solders were marched through the streets while the band played patriotic songs. If there were no band then the soldiers sang or whistled as they marched along. Walter Baker, an agricultural worker from Hawkwell, tells how his call-up did not come until 1916. He was then ordered to report to Warley Barracks and posted to the Middlesex Regiment. Next he was sent to Reading where he did a lot of 'square bashing' and soon learnt that a soldier's life was not as glamorous as he had been led to believe. Crawley was his next camp; here he gained his first experience of living under canvas. There were 20 to a tent and all had to sleep with their feet towards the pole. They had to use their kit bags for pillows and were so tightly packed they could not turn over. With over a thousand soldiers on the site, the ground soon turned to liquid mud and eventually things got so bad that they had to sit up to sleep because the floor of the tent was so

142 Second World War 'Specials', including Harry Frost (back row, second left) and Searles (front row, second right).

wet. With the continuous heavy rain, lack of food and appalling sanitary conditions it was not surprising that there was dysentery and some of his colleagues died. When they complained they were reminded of the soldiers fighting in France whose conditions were considerably worse. When the regiment was eventually moved on to Purfleet, soldiers dropped out beside the road too unfit to march. At least in Purfleet Walter was in barracks with a regular supply of food, mainly stew with dumplings 'as hard as cricket balls' and stewed dried fruit. Tea consisted of bread and jam and any stew left over from earlier in the day, all washed down with tea from the billy can which had also contained the main course!

After several other moves Walter volunteered to work on a farm at Hornchurch. His main job was driving vegetables to Covent Garden by horse and cart. He would leave Hornchurch at 8-9 o'clock at night arriving at Covent Garden between 3-4 a.m. Sometimes he was required to go back again the same day which was an offence as it was illegal to bring a horse into London twice during the course of a single day. When not driving to Covent Garden he worked in the fields wearing his army overcoat and boots—no waterproofs or Wellington boots were provided. Fed up with his situation, he returned to Warley voluntarily and was put on a charge for disobeying Army orders and given 21 days' confinement. Further stints on farms continued and he was eventually sent to Southend, where he learnt to use one of the newly invented tractors and ploughed at Hullbridge, Hockley and Hawkwell.

By now it was 1919 and he was finally sent with his regiment to Germany, sailing up the Rhine to Cologne. A few months later he was discharged and returned to Hawkwell. His memories of Germany were very vivid as he had never been out of England before and he remarked how sorry he felt for the German people.

German Zeppelins were frequently seen in the skies of south-east Essex. In March 1916 the L13, L14 and L15 crossed into England at Southwold, flying at an altitude of 6-7,000 feet. Their targets were the munition factories at Stowmarket, Woolwich and Waltham Abbey. The L13, commanded by Captain Bocker, became separated from its companions and, after dropping high explosives at Springfield near Chelmsford, flew on to the oil refineries at Thames Haven on the Thames, where it dropped five high explosives and 12 incendiaries. Fortunately the tanks were empty and there no casualties. At 1.40 a.m., although damaged, the L13 set out for home, passing over Hawkwell and Rochford.

As the men went off to war, more and more tasks fell to the womenfolk. In Hockley Dolly Dale scandalised the village when she took to driving the milk cart—a most unlady-like activity!

Sadly, at the end of the war there were 30 men from Hockley and Hawkwell who did not come home and whose names are commemorated on a memorial at the Hockley and Hawkwell British Legion at Hawkwell. Casualties continued even after the cessation of hostilities and in Hockley churchyard there is a war grave of a 19-year-old able seaman who died in March 1919, when his ship, the RN trawler *The Ben Alder*, was blown up whilst clearing mines.

In July 1919 Hockley Parish Council held a 'Peace Day' to celebrate the ending of hostilities and a special rate of 2d. was levied to cover the costs. A united service opened the day and afterwards there were sports, tea for all parishioners, a concert and presentation of medals.

Just twenty years later the Second World War broke out. Damage to the area from enemy action was fortunately light, although a mine fell in the vicinity of the Public Hall, another flattened Northlands Farm, Drovers Hill, a V2 rocket crashed in St Peter Road (the crater is still there today) and incendiary bombs rained on Hullbridge. Older residents still recall watching dogfights in the sky during the Battle of Britain.

Local people were supplied with indoor shelters which were of limited use as they only protected the occupants from flying glass and splinters. The air raids presented children with a new hobby—collecting shrapnel—and after raids they would venture out to see what they could find. Some amassed quite sizeable collections of these twisted, and sometimes potentially dangerous, lumps of metal.

Children from the East End of London were evacuated to the relative safety of Hockley and Hawkwell. However, trouble broke out in Hullbridge at the end of the war when the children were returned to their homes. Some of the host families were reluctant to hand back the blankets they had been issued with for the evacuees and the situation was only resolved with difficulty by the authorities.

A searchlight was installed on Plumberow Mount, near the woods, and Hockley School became the Air Raid Patrol headquarters. Manned ARP posts were set up throughout the area: on the Rochford Road, at the junction of Victor Gardens/White Hart Lane, Hawkwell Chase, Pevensey Gardens, High Road, Hockley and near Hullbridge School. An ARP map gives all the telephone contact points in the area and their numbers—Hullbridge post office was Rayleigh 142.

For the men who, for various reasons, could not go off to war, there was the Local Defence Volunteers (LDV), later to be renamed the Home Guard. Hockley lay within the 1st Essex Zone, 1st Essex Battalion, and the first local defence officer was the vicar of Hockley, the Rev. Gardner. The men trained hard, with broomsticks at first before being issued with .36 grenades, Thompson sub-machine carbines and proper uniforms.

The story is told locally of how Captain (later Lieut.-Col.) Wells Jennings, whilst out recruiting in the area for the LDV, called on a woman who had three sons he considered would make useful members of the local detachment. When he told her the purpose of his visit and asked about the eldest son, she replied: 'He's away, sir, working in a factory.' He then asked about the middle one and she said, 'He works at the factory, too, sir.' Finally Captain Wells Jennings enquired about the youngest one and was told, 'He works in a laundry, sir.' The Captain was encouraged by this reply and said cheerily, 'Well, he's just the chap we want. He can help us hang the washing on the Siegfried Line!' The mother responded solemnly, 'Oh, no, sir. You see, he works in the boiler house.'

With an Italian prisoner-of-war camp at nearby Rawreth, it was not unusual to see the prisoners working in the area. They built the Lower Road, Hockley, and were often to be seen employed in Hockley Woods.

Once again there were those who bravely went off to war and did not return. In the graveyard of SS Peter and Paul, Hockley, there are five War Grave Commission graves. Like most communities Hockley has its particular tragedies, one grave being the final resting place for three brothers killed in different theatres of war.

Following their release as German prisoners-of-war, the Graham brothers returned to their home at Francis Farm, Greensward Lane. In memory of those who had died they planted a willow tree on the land next to the farm, and a service of dedication was held. Over the years the tree has grown to be a feature of the lane. The farm has been demolished and replaced by a petrol station—the only one in the country known to include an official war memorial. When the petrol station was redesigned in the 1980s the tree's history came to light and as a result it was protected and incorporated into the design. As Hockley had no war memorial outside of the parish church, the parish council placed a commemorative plaque beneath the tree in 1997 and every Remembrance Sunday the Parish Council assembles with members of the British Legion, a short service is held, and the chairman lays a wreath of poppies.

Chapter Fourteen

From the Vestry to the Fire Station

THE LOCAL GOVERNMENT ACT of 1894 brought into being parish councils, but prior to this, decision making on local affairs had been in the hands of a wealthy and privileged few. These landowners met regularly in the church vestry to decide not only secular, but also ecclesiastical matters relating to the village. Their duties included the collecting of the tithe and the appointment of officers to run the affairs of the village: a waywarden for the highways, an overseer for the poor, the constable and the various church officers such as the churchwarden and sidesmen. In some parishes a dog catcher was also appointed to keep the dogs which accompanied their owners to church in order during services.

In 1840 the method of paying tithes was regulated and the whole of England mapped in the minutest detail with all ownership noted, land holdings (including fields, gardens and woods) measured, and cash values assessed. The tithe map of Hockley makes fascinating reading and notes 3,278 acres of land as arable, 704 acres of meadow and pasture, 97 acres of saltings, 268 acres as common, roads and waste and 16 acres belonging to the church. Hockley Hall is shown next to the church, and the 'village' opposite Bull Woods on the old common. The lands of the parish of Hockley extended to Woodham Ferrers on the north bank of the Crouch and included a small part of Paglesham and, of course, Hullbridge. To demonstrate just how empty this agricultural landscape was 150 years ago, only 13 acres was given over to buildings of any kind. The Commissioners who met at Rayleigh also worked out that the vicar of Hockley had a right to £317 5s. 8d. per annum—a not inconsiderable sum for those days. An additional sum of £953 17s. 2d. was set aside to be used by the parish for the relief of poverty and road mending.

In 1894 the Local Government Act was passed setting out strict rules governing the formation of the new parish councils which it was hoped would encourage the involvement of ordinary people in local affairs. The Act stipulated that the first meeting of the parish council should take place on 4 December 1894 with the new councillors taking up office on the 13th of the month. The selection process was simple: nominations for councillors were invited from all those members of the local community who were on the list of parochial electors. To get on the list, however, an elector had to own land or property in the parish. If they rented—as so many did in those days—they were not eligible to vote. Women, of course, could not stand for election, or vote. The election method as we know it today did not come into being until 1933.

As information on Hawkwell's parish council is not readily to hand what follows relates purely to Hockley.

Such was the enthusiasm in Hockley to become a member of the parish council, that 14 candidates put themselves forward for the seven available places. A meeting of parishioners was therefore held in the schoolroom at Hockley on 23 November 1894, with the purpose of trying to find a way of achieving the required number. The list of candidates was examined and it was noted that it contained six farmers, four tradesmen, three labours and an independent. After considerable discussion it would appear a 'gentlemen's agreement' was arrived at. In order to ensure equitable representation the parish council should comprise two farmers, two tradesmen, two labourers and the independent. The final selection, according to occupation, would take place at the first official meeting of the Hockley Parish Council to be held on 4 December.

When the date finally arrived three of the candidates had dropped out leaving 11 for the seven places. Votes were taken and Charles Lark, who earned his living as a coal dealer and was also licensee of the *Spa Hotel*, withdrew,

143 & 144 Councillor Stephen Harvey one of Hockley's first parish councillors. He served as a councillor for a total of 34 years, 25 of them as chairman. He lived at Kingmans Farm, Hullbridge, seen here *c.*1910. The farmhouse was built on marshes, right against the seawall. Needless to say, the occupants lived in constant fear of inundation as the seawall was considerably lower than it is today.

as did William Sansom, James Harvey and William Lappage. The successful candidates were Stephen Harvey of Kingsmans Farm; George Thorpe of Hanover Farm; Benjamin Moss of Hockley House; Richard Quittenton of St Helens, Hockley; George Clements, owner of the post office; Samuel Gilson, grocer/draper, and William Finch, a marine store dealer. The single seat for the Rochford Rural District Council had also to be filled at this meeting. There were two candidates, Benjamin Moss and Stephen Harvey but Moss withdrew rather than put the parish to the expense of an election.

Mr. Moss was elected chairman with Mr. Quittenden vice-chairman. The schoolmaster, Thomas Day, accepted the position of clerk to the council, although a decision as to his wages was deferred until the next meeting in February 1895, when he was voted a salary of £6 0s. 0d. per annum. Unfortunately none of the clerk's account books remain from the early years of the council, but in 1903 monthly expenditure for March amounted to £3 9s. 0d. It was agreed that the council should meet four times a year, alternating between Hockley and Hullbridge, where it also met in the school.

145 Mr. H.A. Stock (1899-1966), served as clerk to Hockley Parish Council from July 1927 to November 1952, a total of 25 years.

The first business meeting of the council took place at Hullbridge on 21 February 1895, when a Mr. Jackson of Rochford was appointed treasurer. The main agenda item was the ever present problem of the poor water supply at both Hockley and Hullbridge. The members also discussed the distribution of the Hockley Charities which at that time were the responsibility of the parish council, the income being derived from the rent of the Poores Land, then known as Spa Meadow.

One of Hockley's most colourful characters at this time was the Rev. Samuel Maude, vicar of SS Peter and Paul. It would appear that the Rev. Maude was initially no supporter of the new system or the parish council. To make things difficult he refused to hand over the tithe records that had been held by the vestry, and there are constant references in the Parish Council minutes to his lack of co-operation and what to do about it. By 1904, however, he appears to have made his peace with the council and is himself a councillor and vice chairman. In August 1908, Maude was back in the news on account of his reluctance to pay the tithe on some land in his possession. The matter was taken to the Sherriff's Court at Chelmsford for assessment of arrears, where it was heard before a jury. Maude claimed that he had taken the land in as the owner had gone away and it was derelict. The Under Sheriff provoked the court to laughter when he told Maude, 'You will have to do a little husbandry yourself.' Apparently the sum of £1 13s. 7½d. was still outstanding, but as the land was in such a poor state it would take sometime to recover. At the end

146 Hockley firemen in action at a woodyard blaze.

of the hearing the Under Sheriff addressed the jury and told them, 'The case is much ado about nothing', and found in favour of Maude.

The voting arrangements that came into operation in 1933 were very different from those we know today. There were no universal polling hours; they were set by the individual councils to reflect the character of the area and the number of voters on the electors' list. As many people worked on Saturday mornings and had the afternoon free, it was not uncommon for elections to be held on that day and polling stations stayed open from 10 a.m. until 8 p.m. Candidates could not state their political persuasion in their literature, and although many did stand under a political banner, they were described on the ballot paper by their occupation only. In the post-war years it was not unusual to have turn-outs of 70 per cent, which is in sharp contrast to the 30 per cent or less usual in local elections today.

Hullbridge at that time was a ward of the Hockley Parish and it was not until 1966 that it got its own Parish Council. When Hullbridge staged its second election it entered election history. The ballot paper was of exceptional length as 39 people stood for only 12 seats!

When the fire service moved to its new premises in Hawkwell, the fire station became redundant. In the late 1970s the parish council purchased the building and it now houses the offices of the clerk to the council and accommodation for use by the community.

Chapter Fifteen

Mrs. Augusta Mary Tawke and Miss Augusta Saumarez Tawke

HOCKLEY AND HAWKWELL's history would be incomplete without reference to two remarkable women, whose generosity and tireless hard work for the community went a long way towards making the Hockley and Hawkwell of today.

The Tawke family home was originally The Lawns, Rochford, but it would appear that, after she was widowed, Mrs. Augusta Mary Tawke went to live at Whitbreads, Hockley. By this time her daughter, Augusta Saumarez, had set up home for herself just down the road in Bullwood Hall. Both women were passionately interested in the affairs of the local community and it was Mrs. Tawke who purchased two plots of land for £40 from local

147 Whitbreads, Bullwood Hall Lane, Hockley, the home of Mrs. Augusta Mary Tawke. In her old age Miss Augusta Saumarez Tawke also lived at Whitbreads before moving into a smaller residence nearby.

148 Bullwood Hall, Hockley, once the home of Miss Tawke. Now a women's prison.

149 Miss Augusta Saumarez Tawke in old age. Only a small woman, she suffered badly from arthritis, and travelled to Bath to 'take the waters'.

150 The horse trough, on the corner of Fountain Lane and the High Road, Hockley, paid for by Mrs. Tawke. Not only did it offer refreshment for horses, but there was a drinking fountain at the top for human use and a bowl at the bottom for dogs, 1920.

landowner, Samuel Baker, on which to build the public hall. Keeping things in the family her daughter, Augusta Saumarez, was one of the trustees of the charity set up to run the hall, eventually becoming chairman.

When in 1904 a laundry was opened in Bullwood Road to teach young, unemployed women a trade, Mrs. Tawke donated £100 and her daughter paid for all the furnishings. Concerned at the lack of affordable housing for the poor, she built several cottages which were rented out for 4s. 0d. a week.

The water trough and fountain on the corner of Fountain Lane, were also paid for by Mrs. Tawke and donated to the community.

Eventually, well into her '90s, Mrs. Tawke retired to Southend. Her daughter, however, continued her good works and there was hardly a committee or organisation on which she did not serve. During her time she was president of the Women's Institute and Women's Legion, a governor of both Hockley and Hawkwell schools, chairman of the Rochford and Hockley Nursing Association, the Conservative

151 The pulpit in SS Peter and Paul Church, Hockley, carved by Miss Tawke. The panels are decorated with symbols relating to the life of Saint Peter. Photograph taken during the Second World War.

152 The Essex Union Hounds meeting at Rayleigh, a scene Miss Tawke would have known well and enjoyed, *c.*1920.

Association and British Legion Poppy Day organiser. Not surprisingly, as soon as women got the vote, she became a parish councillor and was chairman on two occasions, 1933-8 and 1941-2.

Miss Tawke was also a gifted wood carver and the pulpit in SS Peter and Paul's church, Hockley, is a fine example of her work. She also carved the First World War memorial in the church.

Despite her diminutive size, it is for her equestrian skills that Miss Tawke is most famous, and she published four books in 1934 on her hunting recollections. The books demonstrate only too well the changes that have taken place since her time in the social attitude to hunting. For instance, she writes with pride how the Essex Union Hunt met at Rayleigh and chased a fox through the Rayleigh brickfields, past Turrett House, Hockley, through Bullwood and across to Gusted Hall, Hawkwell. Doubling back, the fox crossed open country to Clements Hall, Hawkwell and from there on to Ashingdon Hall Farm. The chase continued via Canewdon and the Creeksea Ferry, until at Ballards Gore the poor, exhausted creature was eventually caught and killed.

Hares are a very rare sight indeed nowadays in south-east Essex, but in Miss Tawke's time they were literally considered 'fair game'. In her book she tells how the harriers chased one from Hawkwell Hall in a circle via Little Doggetts at Rochford, Ashingdon Church and on to the *White Hart* at Hawkwell, where it was killed. 'A successful day was concluded, with a ball at The Lawns', she writes!

However, there was a more generous side to her nature. When Hawkwell school ran out of needlework material, it was she who supplied it. Like her mother, she was concerned at the lack of housing for the poor and pushed hard for many years, especially when she was on the parish council, for more to be built. Many of the organisations she supported could not have survived without her generous financial contributions and enthusiasm.

Bibliography

Benton, P., *The History of the Rochford Hundred* (1867)
Brown, A.F.J., *Prosperity and Poverty, Rural Essex, 1700-1815* (1996)
Defoe, D., *A Tour Through the Whole Island of Great Britain* (1714-1716)
Francis, E.B., *The Opening of Plumberow Mount* (1914)
Frankland, J., *South Woodham Ferrers, A Pictorial History* (1992)
Granville, A.B. and Phillips, R., *A Brief Account of Hockley Spa Near Southend* (1842)
Jerram-Burrows, L.E., *Bygone Rochford* (1988)
Lane, E.H., *Rayleigh, Its People and Places* (1996)
Lane, E.H. and Fitzgerald, E., *Rayleigh, A Pictorial History* (1991)
Morant, Rev. P., *The History and Antiquities of the County of Essex* (1768)
Rackham, O., *The Woods of South-East Essex* (1986)
Rackham, O., *The History of the Countryside* (1986)
Sorrell, M., *The Peculiar People* (1979)
Tawke, A.S., *Hunting Recollections* (1934)
Tawke, A.S., *Recollections of Southend on Sea and Neighbourhood* (1934)
Watkins, F.J., *A Glimpse into the Past* (1957)

Index

Page numbers in bold refer to illustrations